COLOUR
MOVES

Contents

4   **Foreword**
by Kate Davies

6   **Introduction**
by Claudia Fiocchetti

10   **Foglie Nascoste**
Tam and fingerless gloves

20   **Velino**
Slouch and mitts

26   **Jesi**
Gloves

32   **Gradient Mesh**
Beanie and gauntlets

44 Electric Ups & Downs
Flip-tops

52 Sirente
Mittens

60 Gran Sasso
Slouch and mittens

66 Taighean
Mitts

72 Floral Tapestry
Tam and mittens

82 Majella
Mittens

86 Broken Herringbone
Snood

92 Hypno
Fingerless gloves and mittens

100 Glove blocker templates

104 Resources

105 Abbreviations

Foreword

by Kate Davies

In 2019, KDD held a popular competition for mittens, mitts and glove designs, that later became the *Warm Hands* book. As competition submissions started to come in, one person's work stood out. This person seemed to be using the small canvas of a glove or mitten to explore a set of really innovative design ideas. Graphic patterns danced over the surface of the hands; simple shapes were enlivened with bold colourways; lines and motifs clashed, came together, changed direction. The work was that of Claudia Fiocchetti, and I loved everything that she knitted. Here was someone who evidently had a particular kind of feeling for the potential of stranded colourwork, and whose needles were brimming with fresh ideas.

When it was time for myself and Jeanette Sloan, my co-editor, to select designs from the competition to be commissioned for our book, we kept returning to Claudia's work. We had trouble selecting just one piece: everything that Claudia had submitted, we felt, deserved to be published as a pattern. When it occurred to me that I might be able to find a way of helping her to do just that, the idea for Make // Mark was born.

What makes Claudia's work distinctive is the way that she makes pattern and colour play together. Pattern and colour are literally her livelihood: as an historic painting and stone conservator, she spends each day paying extremely close attention to the details of all kinds of decorative art. Her attentive, creative and emotive approach to colour and pattern is immediately apparent in the 17 designs included here: every element is, quite simply, where it is meant to

be. And, under Claudia's canny hands, the *feeling* of a surface design can shift significantly simply by repositioning a single stitch, or by swapping out one shade for another. Her work truly makes colour *move*.

I have so many personal favourites here: the rhythmic *Electric Ups & Downs*, with their nifty flip-top construction; the *Gradient Mesh* beanie and gauntlets, bringing together colour and line; the playful and beautiful *Foglie Nascoste* set – and the elegant *Jesi* gloves, whose surface patterns echo the play of light over Italy's distinctive diamond-shaped 'bugnato' façades (look them up if you don't know!).

Claudia's colourful patterns – so full of vitality, energy and vim – match the appealing personality of a designer with whom I've enjoyed working enormously over the past year. I think the joy of her work really comes through in the knitting, and I know you are going to love making these beautiful, highly knitterly and eminently wearable accessory designs. One set just won't be enough!

Finally, a word about the imprint under which this book is published: Make // Mark. When, as a fledgling designer of hand-knitting patterns, I began to have ideas for the book that became *Colours of Shetland*, I realised it would be a difficult sell. The book had no definitive genre: neither how-to nor travel writing; not purely knitting, but not cultural history either. I knew an agent was likely to have difficulty representing such a book, and that publishers would struggle finding a suitable place for it on their lists. And, in any case, which commercially-minded publisher would ever take a punt on someone whose capacity for work was severely limited after being disabled by a stroke? So, I decided to make my book myself. I'd had experience of both academic and commercial publishing and had worked for many years as both author and editor. I also had a supportive partner and good friends who were willing to share their professional expertise. So, I put my head down, worked within the means I had, and, over time, produced a book. And, over the years that followed, I produced many more. There are many difficult-to-place books out there, and countless talented writers and designers with wonderful ideas who do not have the same resources or support that I did when taking my first steps on this path. Make // Mark is for them: my way of giving back to an industry which, from those first difficult beginnings, has enabled me not only to develop a new career

in design and publishing but also to build a thriving business that supports many different kinds of creative work. Make // Mark is a not-for-profit enterprise, under which our revenue from book sales is directed into developing the scheme and taking it forward. We are delighted to bring Claudia's book to you. With three more titles already commissioned under this imprint from talented authors and designers, the road ahead promises to be exciting.

Thank you for your support of Make // Mark. We hope that you enjoy this book!

Kate Davies
(on behalf of the KDD team)

Introduction

by Claudia Fiocchetti

I am an Italian/British wall-painting and stone conservator who has always been attracted by art, colour, textiles and crafts in general, as well as by photography and maths. I've found this broad combination of interests to be very useful in my work, as well as in my knitting, which I've always found absorbing, ever since I was a young child who was completely fascinated by how a single thread could become a complete garment. When I was seven, I asked my mum to teach me, and she did so in the English 'throwing' style. From the beginning, I loved the idea of creating textiles to exactly suit one's taste, and knitting has been my go-to hobby throughout my life.

I grew up in Abruzzo, a region of Italy with a very beautiful and inspiring landscape. It rises from

pretty coastal towns, through lakes and gentle hills where grapes are grown for wine, to the Apennine glacier and high peaks of Gran Sasso, which lend their names to designs in this collection. My province (L'Aquila) is often the coldest place in Italy, and I grew up really appreciating the benefit of warm, woollen garments. I still feel that no technical fabric can rival the properties of wool.

A RICH HERITAGE

I moved to the UK in 2008, and feel very lucky that my conservation work has allowed me to connect so meaningfully with Britain's rich cultural heritage and to collaborate with so many wonderful and welcoming institutions. Working at places like William Morris's Red House in Bexleyheath has allowed me to develop a deep understanding of the important history of British applied arts, as well as their links to Italian decorative traditions, which always feel familiar and close to me. I love walking – and, though I enjoy city life, I find the rural landscapes of England, Wales and Scotland very inspiring. I've broadened my horizons in so many different ways since moving to the UK, and the landscape of my knitting has greatly expanded too! Through English books, the Internet, my local knitting club, and personal friends, I have gradually become a designer of patterns whose knitting brain now 'thinks' in English (though I certainly intend to translate my work into Italian in the future). I'm proud of my bilingual, bicultural perspective, which is a unique part of who I am as a person, and as a hand-knit designer too.

Since I was very young, I've drawn huge amounts of inspiration from the decorative arts, and have always loved ancient geometric mosaics and medieval wall-painting in particular. I find many areas of confluence between figurative art and textile design, and often draw on such connections in my knitting, where I'm particularly inspired by repetitive, graphic patterns and motifs. Travelling (for both work and fun) also continually feeds my imagination. Often, it amazes me to find such close connections between local landscapes and people, their textiles and their crafts. I have experienced this epiphany very strongly in places like Peru and Mexico and, most recently, in Shetland. In this collection, you'll find inspiration from my travels in designs like *Taighean* and *Sirente*.

MOTION AND EMOTION

Like many visual people, I often find that I 'think' in pattern, and I'm continually fascinated by the bold and playful effects that can be achieved by the rhythmic repetition of simple, graphic motifs, whether I'm doodling on the phone or examining tiles, carpets or architectural façades, such as those of the Palazzo Ricci, which inspired the *Jesi* gloves in this collection. I also adore colour, and love many different juxtapositions and combinations, including shades of grey and black that are never really monochrome, but are rather always full of colour in themselves. Graphic patterns, repetitive motifs and simple shapes tend to provide the conceptual 'frame' of my design work, but it is always colour that makes my patterns spring to life and develop their own particular vitality. Patterns and motifs create the rhythm of my work, but truly – colour makes it move! I hope you'll see this vital interplay between pattern and colour in many designs in this collection – but it's perhaps easiest to perceive in the *Foglie Nascoste* (Hidden Leaves) tam and gloves. Here, simply experimenting with the 'foreground' and 'background' shades that I'd used to define a familiar floral motif allowed a completely different pattern to appear. With a simple shift in colour, from behind the flowers emerged the hidden leaves.

The name of my collection – *Colour Moves* – is intended to capture that doubled sense of rhythm and feeling, motion and emotion that I often experience when working with pattern. I hope this is something that those who knit my designs are able to feel as well.

CREATING A COLLECTION

So, how did I happen to create the *Colour Moves* collection? Well, I've been developing and self-publishing my own patterns in a rather ad-hoc fashion since 2015. Then, at the start of 2019, I decided to take part in KDD's annual competition, in which designers were invited to submit pattern ideas for gloves, mitts and mittens. One of my submissions – *Blue Interference* – was then chosen by Kate Davies and Jeanette Sloan to be published in their *Warm Hands* collection: a beautiful book of patterns created by talented designers from many different backgrounds all over the world. I felt really encouraged by having my work selected, and the experience of developing a pattern for *Warm Hands* helped me to gain confidence in my work, pushing me to experiment with design ideas, to give

shape to several concepts I'd had stored in my mind for a long time, and to generate bold ideas for new patterns to take forward. The response of my fellow knitters in the *Warm Hands* competition and KDD Ravelry group was very enabling and positive, and a personal conversation with Kate finally encouraged me to take the first steps, with her help, towards publishing my own collection of original accessory designs.

When Kate explained to me the purpose of Make // Mark – a scheme to support the development and publication of the work of new and emerging creative talent – I felt very excited and extremely honoured to be the first designer whose work would appear under this new imprint. But that initial excitement was nothing compared to the deeply rewarding process of seeing my book take shape over the weeks and months that followed, with the support of Kate and her wonderful team. I've knitted many different samples; I've learned how to work to a style template and develop charts that are easy to read and follow. I've considered aspects of pattern and book design I'd never thought about before, such as how a glove eventually gets to fit on a printed page, and what kinds of images

and information might be necessary to support a set of clear instructions.

I can't give enough thanks to all the people who have supported me in various ways during the preparation of this book. First of all to Kate, for whom I feel great admiration; to Melanie Patton, who always handles my many yarn shipments with kind efficiency; to Tom Barr, for his wonderful photographic and graphic design skills; to Sam Kilday, for his help in the studio and with styling; to KDD's fantastic models, Jane Hunter and Fenella Pole; and to technical editor Frauke Urban, with whom it is always a pleasure to work.

And finally, I would like to thank my all family and friends who have encouraged me throughout the process. In particular, I must express warm gratitude to my mum, to whom I am dedicating this book, not merely to fulfil a familiar Italian stereotype, but because she has always been (and remains) my biggest fan and supporter throughout my life. Thank you, Mum.

In the pages that follow, you'll find 17 individual accessory designs in two beautiful (and very different) KDD yarns: fingering-weight Milarrochy Tweed, and Aran-weight Àrd-Thìr. Many designs, like *Floral Tapestry*, *Gradient Mesh* or *Gran Sasso*, are accessory 'sets' designed to be worn together, but whose individual components look equally good as separates. You'll also find bold stand-alone patterns like *Hypno* or *Jesi* together with *Broken Herringbone* (a long snood that can be cosily wrapped twice around the neck), and *Electric Ups & Downs*, a rhythmically patterned pair of flip-top mittens featuring an innovative construction that I really enjoyed developing. There are patterns for small hands and large; beanies, tams and slouchy hats; mittens and mitts; full-finger or half-finger gloves; and longer gauntlets. Where relevant, patterns include full and comprehensive charts – and many individual designs include suggestions for alternative palettes, encouraging you to experiment and play with the movement of colour, just as I like to do. And, to provide the final finishing touch for your work, you'll also find a tutorial and template to create your very own set of glove and mitten blockers. I've loved developing the *Colour Moves* collection, and my final wish is for these patterns to bring joy to you and many other knitters!

Thank you

Claudia Fiocchetti

FOGLIE NASCOSTE

This pattern is based on a geometrical floral motif that I have been drawing since childhood. When I half-shifted the repeat, against a light green (Stockiemuir) background I found a surprising leafy pattern stood out more than the original floral motif. "Foglie Nascoste" means "hidden leaves" in Italian - a fitting name for this design!

FOGLIE NASCOSTE TAM

YARN

Kate Davies Designs Milarrochy Tweed (70% Wool; 30% Mohair; 100m / 109yds per 25g ball)
1 ball of each of the following shades:
A Garth
B Stockiemuir
C Buckthorn
D Tarbet
E Ardlui
F Gloamin'

NEEDLES AND NOTIONS

Gauge-size needle(s) of your preferred type for working in the round
Below gauge-size needle(s) of your preferred type for working in the round
Gauge-size needle(s) of your preferred type for working small circumferences (for crown top)
Stitch markers
Tapestry needle

GAUGE

32 stitches and 36 rounds to 10cm / 4in over stranded colourwork in the round on gauge-size needle(s)
Use 3mm needle(s) as a starting point for swatching.

SIZE

To fit adult head with 51-53.5cm / 20-21in circumference

PATTERN NOTES

This neatly-fitting tam is worked from bottom to top. After the corrugated rib brim, the tam body is worked in stranded colourwork.

CHART NOTES

Read from right to left throughout. After brim, repeat chart 6 times across each round.

INSTRUCTIONS

1

CAST ON, WORK BRIM

With shade A, below gauge-size needle(s), and using long-tail cast on (or your preferred method) cast on 130 sts, pm, and join for working in the round.

Round 1: Reading chart from right to left, join in B, and work in 1x1 twisted rib as foll: (K1tblA, p1B) around.

Following chart, work rounds 2-12. *12 rounds worked*

Break A and weave in tail on next round.

2

WORK TAM BODY

Change to gauge-size needle(s) and with B work increases over round 13 as foll:

Round 13: (K3, m1, k2, m1) 25 times, k5. *50 sts inc; 180 sts*

Rounds 14-55: Working chart from right to left, repeating chart 6 times across each round, and changing shades where indicated, work chart rounds 14-55.

3

WORK CROWN

With shades A and B, work decreases as charted over rounds 56-84, shifting to gauge-size needle(s) of your preferred type for working small circumferences as crown reduces in size. Break yarn. Draw up through remaining 6 sts, draw down through centre and fasten off to WS of work.

4

FINISHING

Weave in all ends to the back of the work. Soak tam in cool water for 20 minutes to allow stitches to relax and bloom. Press dry between towels. Shape tam over a 24 cm / 9½in diameter plate and leave to fully dry.

Enjoy your Foglie Nascoste tam!

CHART

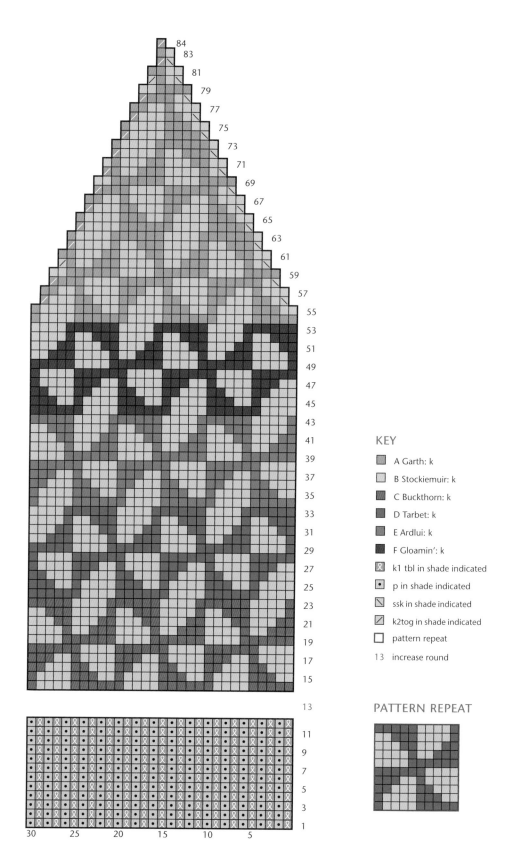

KEY

- A Garth: k
- B Stockiemuir: k
- C Buckthorn: k
- D Tarbet: k
- E Ardlui: k
- F Gloamin': k
- k1 tbl in shade indicated
- p in shade indicated
- ssk in shade indicated
- k2tog in shade indicated
- pattern repeat
- 13 increase round

PATTERN REPEAT

FOGLIE NASCOSTE FINGERLESS GLOVES

Make yourself a matching set with the Foglie Nascoste tam!

YARN

Kate Davies Designs Milarrochy Tweed (70% Wool; 30% Mohair; 100m / 109yds per 25g ball)
1 ball of each of the following shades:
A Garth
B Stockiemuir
C Buckthorn
D Tarbet
E Ardlui
F Gloamin'

NEEDLES AND NOTIONS

Gauge-size needle(s) of your preferred type for working small circumferences
Below gauge-size needle(s) of your preferred type for working small circumferences
Gauge-size needle(s) of your preferred type for working fingers
Long gauge-size circular needles or holders for holding finger stitches
Waste yarn (for holding thumb stitches)
Stitch markers
Tapestry needle

GAUGE

32 stitches and 36 rounds to 10cm / 4in over stranded colourwork in the round on gauge-size needle(s)
Use 3mm needle(s) as a starting point for swatching.

SIZE

To fit adult hand with 18-20.5cm / 7-8in circumference

PATTERN NOTES

These fingerless gloves are worked from bottom to top. After the corrugated rib cuff, the hand is worked in stranded colourwork. Waste yarn is added for an afterthought thumb and the four half-fingers and thumb are worked separately, each one in a different shade of yarn.

CHART NOTES

Repeat chart twice across each round and read from right to left throughout. Note the oppositional thumb placement for right and left hands.

INSTRUCTIONS

1 CAST ON, WORK CUFF

With shade A, below gauge-size needle(s), and using long-tail cast on (or your preferred method) cast on 60 sts, pm, and join for working in the round.
Round 1: Reading chart from right to left, join in B, and work in 1x1 twisted rib as foll: (K1tblA, p1B) around.
Following chart, work rounds 2-15. *15 rounds worked*

2 WORK HAND

Change to gauge-size needle(s), and, working chart from right to left, repeating chart twice across each round, and changing shades where indicated work chart rounds 16-40.

3 PLACE THUMB

Right Hand
Round 41: K1 in pattern, k9 with waste yarn, return last 9 sts to lh needle, then, with working yarn, work across these sts in pattern, and complete round as est.

Left Hand
Round 41: K20 in pattern, k9 with waste yarn, return last 9 sts to lh needle, then, with working yarn, work across these sts in pattern, and complete round as est.

4 COMPLETE HAND

Work rounds 42-66 as est. Break B. (When working right hand, do not break F - this shade is used next).

5 HALF FINGERS

Right Hand
Index finger
With F and gauge-size needle(s), work index finger as foll:
Round 1: K9 sts, using backward-loop cast on, cast on 1 st in the gap between fingers, sl21 sts to holder or spare needle (palm), sl21 sts to a second holder (back of hand), k9, pm, and join for working in the round. *19 sts*
Rounds 2-9: K19.
Round 10: Bind off. Break yarn.

Middle finger
With A and gauge-size needle(s), work middle finger as foll:
Round 1: Sl8 sts from palm sts holder, k8, using backward-loop cast on, cast on 1 st in the gap between fingers, sl8 sts from back of hand sts holder, k8, using backward-loop cast on, cast on 1 st in the gap between fingers, pm, and join for working in the round. *18 sts*
Rounds 2-9: K18.
Round 10: Bind off.

Ring finger
With D and gauge-size needle(s), work ring finger as foll:
Round 1: Sl7 sts from palm sts holder, k7, using backward-loop cast on, cast on 1 st in the gap between fingers, sl7 sts from back of hand sts holder, k7, using backward-loop cast on, cast on 1 st in the gap between fingers, pm, and join for working in the round. *16 sts*
Rounds 2-9: K16.
Round 10: Bind off.

Little finger
With C and gauge-size needle(s), work little finger as foll:
Round 1: Sl the last 6 sts from palm sts holder, k6, sl the last 6 sts from back of hand sts holder, k6, using backward-loop cast on, cast on 2 sts in the gap between fingers, pm, and join for working in the round. *14 sts*
Rounds 2-9: K14.
Round 10: Bind off.

Left Hand
Little finger
With C and gauge-size needle(s), work little finger as foll:
Round 1: K6, using backward-loop cast on, cast on 2 sts in the gap between fingers, sl24 sts to holder or spare needle (palm), sl24 sts to a second holder (back of hand), k6, pm, and join for working in the round. *14 sts*
Rounds 2-9: K14.
Round 10: Bind off.

Ring finger
With D and gauge-size needle(s), work ring finger as follow:
Round 1: Sl7 sts from palm sts holder, k7, using backward-loop cast on, cast on 1 st in the gap between fingers, sl7 sts from back of hand sts holder, k7, using backward-loop cast on, cast on 1 st in the gap between fingers, pm, and join for

working in the round. *16 sts*
Rounds 2-9: K16.
Round 10: Bind off.

Middle finger

With A and gauge-size needle(s), work middle finger as foll:
Round 1: Sl8 sts from palm sts holder, k8, using backward-loop cast on, cast on 1 st in the gap between fingers, sl8 sts from back of hand sts holder, k8, using backward-loop cast on, cast on 1 st in the gap between fingers, pm, and join for working in the round. *18 sts*
Rounds 2-9: K18.
Round 10: Bind off.

Index finger

With F and gauge-size needle(s), work index finger as foll:
Round 1: Sl the last 9 sts from palm sts holder, k9, sl the last 9 sts from back of hand sts holder, k9, using backward-loop cast on, cast on 1 st in the gap between fingers, pm, and join for working in the round. *19 sts*
Rounds 2-9: K19.
Round 10: Bind off.

6

COMPLETE THUMB

Carefully remove waste yarn and sl18 sts to gauge-size needle(s).
Round 1: With E, K9, puk1 st in the gap where thumb meets palm, k9, puk1 st in the gap, pm, and join for working in the round. *20 sts*
Rounds 2-9: K20.
Round 10: Bind off.

Make a second glove to match.

7

FINISHING

Weave in all ends to the back of the work, using yarn ends to carefully close any remaining gaps at the base of fingers and thumb. Soak gloves in cool water for 20 minutes to allow stitches to relax and bloom. Press dry between towels. Shape gloves using glove blockers (if you have them) or pins to position thumb and fingers. Dry flat, and leave to fully dry.

Enjoy your Foglie Nascoste fingerless gloves!

CHART

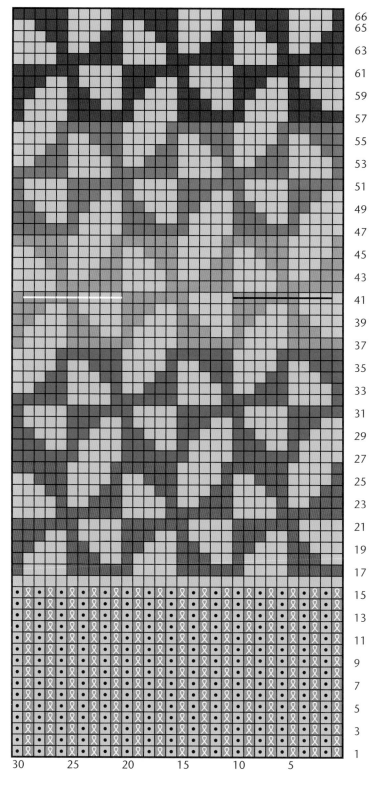

66
65
63
61
59
57
55
53
51
49
47
45
43
41
39
37
35
33
31
29
27
25
23
21
19
17
15
13
11
9
7
5
3
1

30   25   20   15   10   5

KEY

	A Garth: k
	B Stockiemuir: k
	C Buckthorn: k
	D Tarbet: k
	E Ardlui: k
	F Gloamin': k
⧄	k1 tbl in shade indicated
⊡	p in shade indicated
	k with waste yarn, then in shade indicated (left hand)
	k with waste yarn, then in shade indicated (right hand)
☐	pattern repeat

PATTERN REPEAT

VELINO

Above my birth town of Avezzano (in the Italian region of Abruzzo) sits the mountain of Velino, standing at 2,487m high. In winter Velino is frequently capped with snow and in summer, the rocks that cover its surface gleam in the sunlight, rough and white. The colour and texture of this hat and mitts set recalls the mountainous landscape of my childhood.

VELINO SLOUCH

YARN

Kate Davies Designs Àrd-Thìr (60% Peruvian Highland Wool; 40% Alpaca; 65m / 71yds per 50g skein)

Kiloran: 3 x 50g skeins

(If making the Velino hat and mitts set, you can comfortably do so with 4 skeins of Àrd-Thìr.)

NEEDLES AND NOTIONS

Gauge-size needle(s) of your preferred type for working in the round

Below gauge-size needle(s) of your preferred type for working in the round

Stitch markers

Tapestry needle

GAUGE

22 stitches and 26 rounds to 10cm / 4in over pattern in the round on gauge-size needle(s)

Use 4.5mm needle(s) as a starting point for swatching.

SIZE

To fit adult head with 51-56cm / 20-22in circumference

This hat is quite roomy, so should accommodate most adult sizes.

PATTERN NOTES

This hat is worked in the round from bottom to top with an optional pom-pom added at the end.

INSTRUCTIONS

1   CAST ON, WORK BRIM

With below gauge-size needle(s), and using long-tail cast on (or your preferred method), cast on 88 sts, pm, and join for working in the round.
Round 1-6: (K2, p2) around (2x2 rib).

2   WORK HAT BODY

Change to gauge-size needle(s), and on the next round, increase as foll:
Round 7: [(K4, m1) 10 times, k4] twice. *20 sts inc; 108 sts*
Round 8: (K2, p2) around.
Round 9: P1, *k2, p2; repeat from * to last 3 sts, k2, p1.
Repeat rounds 8 and 9 21 more times. *51 rounds worked*

3   WORK CROWN

Round 52: (K1, p2tog, p1) around. *27 sts dec; 81 sts rem*
Round 53: (K1, p2tog) around. *27 sts dec; 54 sts rem*
Round 54: (K2tog) around. *27 sts dec; 27 sts rem*
Round 55: K1, *k2tog; repeat from * to end of round. *13 sts dec; 14 sts rem*
Round 56: (K2tog) around. *7 sts dec; 7 sts rem*
Break yarn. Draw yarn up through remaining 7 sts, draw down through centre and fasten off to WS of work.

4   POMPOM (OPTIONAL)

With your remaining yarn, make a pompom of your preferred size, and securely fasten to the top of the hat crown.

5   FINISHING

Weave in all ends to the back of the work. Soak hat in cool water for 20 minutes to allow stitches to relax and bloom. Press dry between towels. Shape hat, using as blocker a head mannequin or simply a balloon blown in the right size, leave to fully dry.

Enjoy your Velino slouch!

VELINO MITTS

Make yourself a matching set with the Velino slouch!

YARN

Kate Davies Designs Àrd-Thìr (60% Peruvian Highland Wool; 40% Alpaca; 65m / 71yds per 50g skein)
Kiloran: 2 x 50g skeins
(If making the Velino hat and mitts set, you can comfortably do so with 4 skeins of Àrd-Thìr.)

NEEDLES AND NOTIONS

Gauge-size needle(s) of your preferred type for working small circumferences
Below gauge-size needle(s) of your preferred type for working small circumferences
Waste yarn (for holding thumb stitches)
Stitch markers
Tapestry needle

GAUGE

22 stitches and 26 rounds to 10cm / 4in over pattern in the round on gauge-size needle(s)
Use 4.5mm needle(s) as a starting point for swatching.

SIZE

To fit adult hand with 18-20.5cm / 7-8in circumference

PATTERN NOTES

These mittens are worked from bottom to top with an integrated thumb gusset.

INSTRUCTIONS

1 CAST ON, WORK CUFF

With below gauge-size needle(s), and using long-tail cast on (or your preferred method), cast on 36 sts, pm, and join for working in the round.
Round 1-12: (K2, p2) around.

2 WORK HAND

Change to gauge-size needle(s) and work the mitten body as foll:
Round 13: (K2, p2) around.
Round 14: P1, *k2, p2; repeat from * to last 3 sts, k2, p1.
Rounds 15-26: Repeat rounds 13 and 14 6 more times.

3 WORK THUMB GUSSET

Round 27: (K2, p2) 4 times, k2, pm, m1, pm, p2, (k2, p2) 4 times. *1 st inc; 37 sts*
Round 28: P1, (k2, p2) 4 times, k1, slm, k1, slm, k1, (p2, k2) 4 times, p1.
Round 29: (K2, p2) 4 times, k2, slm, m1, k1, m1, slm, p2, (k2, p2) 4 times. *2 sts inc; 39 sts*
Round 30: P1, (k2, p2) 4 times, k1, slm, k2, p1, slm, k1, (p2, k2) 4 times, p1.
Round 31: (K2, p2) 4 times, k2, slm, m1, p1, k2, m1, slm, p2, (k2, p2) 4 times. *2 sts inc; 41 sts*
Round 32: P1, (k2, p2) 4 times, k1, slm, p1, k2, p2, slm, k1, (p2, k2) 4 times, p1.
Round 33: (K2, p2) 4 times, k2, slm, m1, p2, k2, p1, m1, slm, p2, (k2, p2) 4 times. *2 sts inc; 43 sts*
Round 34: P1, (k2, p2) 4 times, k1, slm, p2, k2, p2, k1, slm, k1, (p2, k2) 4 times, p1.
Round 35: (K2, p2) 4 times, k2, slm, m1, k1, p2, k2, p2, m1, slm, p2, (k2, p2) 4 times. *2 sts inc; 45 sts*
Round 36: P1, (k2, p2) 4 times, k1, slm, k1, p2, k2, p2, k2, slm, k1, (p2, k2) 4 times, p1.
Round 37: (K2, p2) 4 times, k2, slm, m1, (k2, p2) twice, k1, m1, slm, p2, (k2, p2) 4 times. *2 sts inc; 47 sts*
Round 38: P1, (k2, p2) 4 times, k1, slm, (k2, p2) twice, k2, p1, slm, k1, (p2, k2) 4 times, p1.
Round 39: (K2, p2) 4 times, k2, rm, slip 11 gusset sts to waste yarn, m1, rm, p2, (k2, p2) 4 times. *36 sts rem*

4 COMPLETE HAND

Round 40: Repeat round 14.
Rounds 41-50: Repeat rounds 13-14 5 more times.

5 WORK TOP RIB

Change to below gauge-size needle(s) and complete the top of the hand as foll:
Rounds 51-54: (K2, p2) around (2x2 rib).
Round 55: Bind off. Break yarn.

6 COMPLETE THUMB

With gauge-size needle(s), work thumb as foll:
Slip 11 gusset sts from waste yarn to gauge-size needle(s), puk1 in the gap where thumb meets palm, pm, and join for working in the round. *12 sts*
Round 1-4: (K2, p2) around (2x2 rib).
Round 5: Bind off. Break yarn.

Make a second mitt to match.

7 FINISHING

Weave in all ends to the back of the work, using yarn ends to carefully close any remaining gaps at thumb base. Soak mitts in cool water for 20 minutes to allow stitches to relax and bloom. Press dry between towels. Shape mittens using glove blockers (if you have them) or pins to position thumb. Dry flat, and leave to fully dry.

Enjoy your Velino mitts!

J E S I

This design is based on a two-colour motif, inspired by the diamond ashlar patterns of many Italian historic facades, such as the Palazzo Ricci in Jesi. I rotated the square motif 45°, creating an equilateral rhomboid, which I then divided in two: half in light, half in shade. Adding a smaller rhomboid motif, in which light and shade are swapped, lends an interesting 3D effect to this rhythmic pattern.

JESI

YARN
Kate Davies Designs Milarrochy Tweed (70% Wool; 30% Mohair; 100m / 109yds per 25g ball)
A Lochan: 2 x 25g balls
B Smirr: 1 x 25g ball

NEEDLES AND NOTIONS
Gauge-size needle(s) of your preferred type for working small circumferences
Below gauge-size needle(s) of your preferred type for working small circumferences
Gauge-size needle(s) of your preferred type for working fingers
Long gauge-size circular needles or holders for holding finger stitches
Waste yarn (for holding thumb stitches)
Stitch markers
Tapestry needle

GAUGE
32 stitches and 36 rounds to 10cm / 4in over stranded stockinette in the round on gauge-size needle(s)
Use 3mm needle(s) as a starting point for swatching.

SIZE
To fit adult hand with 18-20.5cm / 7-8in circumference

SPECIAL TECHNIQUES
Picot hem
The following tutorial may be useful:
https://www.youtube.com/watch?v=NIPB_u1KjY8

PATTERN NOTES
These gloves are worked from bottom to top. After a cuff with a turned picot hem, the hand is completed in stranded colourwork, with an afterthought thumb. The four fingers are completed, and the thumb is worked separately at the end. The length of the fingers can easily be adjusted, as required.

CHART NOTES
Read chart from right to left throughout, paying attention to the thumb positioning for right and left hands, and repeating chart twice across each round.

INSTRUCTIONS

1 CAST ON, WORK CUFF

With shade A, below gauge-size needle(s), and long-tail cast on (or your preferred method) cast on 60 sts, pm, and join for working in the round.
Rounds 1-11: K.
Round 12: Join in B, k.
Round 13: Picot round: with B, (k2tog, yo) around. *60 sts*
Round 14: K. Break B.
Rounds 15-24: With A, k.
Round 25: Joining round: with spare below gauge-size needle, pu (without knitting) 60 sts around cast-on edge (slipping loops of cast on to needle). Fold hem to inside of work along row of yos on round 13; place needles parallel to one another, and with working yarn, *k 1 st from front needle together with 1 st from back needle; repeat from * to end of round.

2 WORK HAND

Rounds 26-57: Change to gauge-size needle(s), and, working chart from right to left, changing shades where indicated, and repeating chart twice across each round, work chart rounds 26-57.

3 PLACE THUMB

Right Hand
Round 58: K1 in pattern, k9 with waste yarn, return last 9 sts to lh needle, then, with working yarn, work across these sts in pattern, and complete round as est.

Left Hand
Round 58: K20 in pattern, k9 with waste yarn, return last 9 sts to lh needle, then, with working yarn, work across these sts in pattern, and complete round as est.

4 COMPLETE HAND

Rounds 59-83: Work in pattern.
Break yarn B.

5 WORK FINGERS

Right Hand
Index Finger
With A and gauge-size needle(s), work index finger as foll:
Round 1: K9 sts, using backward-loop cast on, cast on 1 st in the gap between fingers, sl21 sts to holder or spare needle (palm), sl21 sts to a second holder (back of hand), k9, pm, and join for working in the round. *19 sts*
Rounds 2-25: K19.
Round 26: K1, *k2tog; repeat from * to end of round. *9 sts dec; 10 sts rem*
Round 27: (K2tog) around. *5 sts dec; 5 sts rem*
Break yarn. Draw yarn up through remaining 5 sts, draw down through centre and fasten off to WS.

Middle Finger
With A and gauge-size needle(s), work middle finger as foll:
Round 1: Sl8 sts from palm sts holder, k8, using backward-loop cast on, cast on 1 st in the gap between fingers, sl8 sts from back of hand sts holder, k8, using backward-loop cast on, cast on 1 st in the gap between fingers, pm, and join for working in the round. *18 sts*
Rounds 2-28: K18.
Round 29: (K2tog) around. *9 sts dec; 9 sts rem*
Round 30: K1, *k2tog; repeat from * to end of round. *4 sts dec; 5 sts rem*
Break yarn. Draw yarn up through remaining 5 sts, draw down through centre and fasten off to WS.

Ring Finger
With A and gauge-size needle(s), work ring finger as foll:
Round 1: Sl7 sts from palm sts holder, k7, using backward-loop cast on, cast on 1 st in the gap between fingers, sl7 sts from back of hand sts holder, k7, using backward-loop cast on, cast on 1 st in the gap between fingers, pm, and join for working in the round. *16 sts*
Rounds 2-25: K16.
Round 26: (K2tog) around. *8 sts dec; 8 sts rem*
Round 27: (K2tog) around. *4 sts dec; 4 sts rem*
Break yarn. Draw yarn up through remaining 4 sts, draw down through centre and fasten off to WS.

Little Finger
With A and gauge-size needle(s), work little finger as foll:
Round 1: Sl the last 6 sts from palm sts holder, k6, sl the last 6 sts from back of hand sts holder, k6, using backward-loop cast on, cast on 2 sts in the gap between fingers, pm, and join for working in the round. *14 sts*

Rounds 2-18: K14.
Round 19: (K2tog) around. *7 sts dec; 7 sts rem*
Round 20: K1, *k2tog; repeat from * to end of round. *3 sts dec; 4 sts rem*
Break yarn. Draw yarn up through remaining 4 sts, draw down through centre and fasten off to WS.

Left Hand
Little Finger
With A and gauge-size needle(s), work little finger as foll:
Round 1: K6, using backward-loop cast on, cast on 2 sts in the gap between fingers, sl24 sts to holder or spare needle (palm), sl24 sts to a second holder (back of hand), k6, pm, and join for working in the round. *14 sts*
Rounds 2-18: K14.
Round 19: (K2tog) around. *7 sts dec; 7 sts rem*
Round 20: K1, *k2tog; repeat from * to end of round. *3 sts dec; 4 sts rem*
Break yarn. Draw yarn up through remaining 4 sts, draw down through centre and fasten off to WS.

Ring Finger
With A and gauge-size needle(s), work ring finger as foll:
Round 1: Sl7 sts from palm sts holder, k7, using backward-loop cast on, cast on 1 st in the gap between fingers, sl7 sts from back of hand sts holder, k7, using backward-loop cast on, cast on 1 st in the gap between fingers, pm, and join for working in the round. *16 sts*
Rounds 2-25: K16.
Round 26: (K2tog) around. *8 sts dec; 8 sts rem*
Round 27: (K2tog) around. *4 sts dec; 4 sts rem*
Break yarn. Draw yarn up through remaining 4 sts, draw down through centre and fasten off to WS.

Middle Finger
With A and gauge-size needle(s), work middle finger as foll:
Round 1: Sl8 sts from palm sts holder, k8, using backward-loop cast on, cast on 1 st in the gap between fingers, sl8 sts from back of hand sts holder, k8, using backward-loop cast on, cast on 1 st in the gap between fingers, pm, and join for working in the round. *18 sts*
Rounds 2-28: K18.
Round 29: (K2tog) around. *9 sts dec; 9 sts rem*
Round 30: K1, *k2tog; repeat from * to end of round. *4 sts dec; 5 sts rem*
Break yarn. Draw yarn up through remaining 5 sts,

draw down through centre and fasten off to WS.
Index Finger
With A and gauge-size needle(s), work index finger as foll:
Round 1: Sl the last 9 sts from palm sts holder, k9, sl the last 9 sts from back of hand sts holder, k9, using backward-loop cast on, cast on 1 st in the gap between fingers, pm, and join for working in the round. *19 sts*
Rounds 2-25: K19.
Round 26: K1, *k2tog; repeat from * to end of round. *9 sts dec; 10 sts rem*
Round 27: (K2tog) around. *5 sts dec; 5 sts rem*
Break yarn. Draw yarn up through remaining 5 sts, draw down through centre and fasten off to WS.

WORK THUMB

Carefully remove waste yarn and sl18 sts to gauge-size needle(s).
Round 1: With A, *k9, puk2 in the gap where thumb meets palm*, repeat from * once, pm, and join for working in the round. *22 sts*
Rounds 2-6: K22.
Round 7: (K9, k2tog) 2 times. *2 sts dec; 20 sts rem*
Rounds 8-25: K20.
Round 26: (K2tog) around. *5 sts dec; 10 sts rem*
Round 27: (K2tog) around. *5 sts dec; 5 sts rem*
Break yarn. Draw yarn up through remaining 5 sts, draw down through centre and fasten off to WS.

Make a second glove to match.

7   FINISHING

Weave in all ends to the back of the work, using yarn ends to carefully close any remaining gaps at the base of fingers and thumb. Soak gloves in cool water for 20 minutes to allow stitches to relax and bloom. Press dry between towels. Shape gloves using glove blockers (if you have them) or pins to position thumb and fingers. Dry flat, and leave to fully dry.

Enjoy your Jesi gloves!

CHART

KEY

■ A Lochan: k

□ B Smirr: k

▨ k2tog in shade indicated

▣ yarnover in shade indicated

▨ k with waste yarn, then in shade indicated (left hand)

▨ k with waste yarn, then in shade indicated (right hand)

□ pattern repeat

PATTERN REPEAT

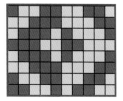

GRADIENT MESH

A colourful pattern set of beanie and gauntlets, featuring a doubled-square motif, which highlights a beautiful gradient of 8 shades of Milarrochy Tweed across a neutral background.

GRADIENT MESH BEANIE

YARN

Kate Davies Designs Milarrochy Tweed (70% Wool; 30% Mohair; 100m / 109yds per 25g ball).

Two balls of **A** Birkin and one ball of each of the following shades:

B Campion	**F** Ardlui
C Gloamin	**G** Garth
D Lochan'	**H** Stockiemuir
E Tarbet	**I** Cowslip

NEEDLES AND NOTIONS

Gauge-size needle(s) of your preferred type (for hat body)
Gauge-size needles of your preferred type for working small circumferences (for crown)
Below gauge-size needle(s) of your preferred type (for brim)
Stitch markers
Tapestry needle

GAUGE

32 stitches and 36 rounds to 10cm / 4in over stranded colourwork in the round on gauge-size needle(s)
Use 3mm needle(s) as a starting point for swatching.

SIZE

To fit adult head with 51-56cm / 20-22in circumference

PATTERN NOTES

This hat is knitted from bottom to top. After the brim, the hat body is worked in stranded colourwork, with an optional pompom added at the end. Pay close attention to shade changes and the position of purl stitches when working the brim.

CHART NOTES

Read from right to left throughout, repeating chart 8 times across each round (for brim) and 10 times across each round (for hat body).

INSTRUCTIONS

1 CAST ON, WORK BRIM

With shade A, below gauge needle(s), and long-tail cast on (or your preferred method) cast on 128 sts, pm, and join for working in the round.
Rounds 1-17: Reading chart from right to left, and changing shades where indicated, work in 1x1 rib as foll: (K1, p1) around.

2 WORK HAT BODY

Change to gauge-size needle(s) and with A work increase round 18 as foll:
Round 18: K2, m1, *k4, m1; repeat from * to last 2 sts before marker, k2. *32 sts inc; 160 sts*
Working chart from right to left and changing shades where indicated, begin working beanie body from round 19.
Rounds 19-70: Working chart from right to left, and repeating chart 10 times across each round work rounds 19-70.

3 WORK CROWN

Rounds 71-73: Work crown shaping, changing shades, working decreases, and shifting to smaller needles as crown circumference reduces. *40 sts dec; 120 sts rem*
Round 74: Work in pattern. At end of round, move marker as foll:
Rm, sl the last st on rh needle to lh needle, pm.
Round 75: K2tog (working the last st of round 74 tog with first st of round 75) work from chart to end of round. *20 sts dec; 100 sts rem*
Rounds 76-83: Work from chart as est. *90 sts dec; 10 sts rem*
Break yarn. Draw yarn up through remaining 10 sts, draw down through centre and fasten off to WS of work.

4 POMPOM (OPTIONAL)

Using all the shades, make a pompom of your preferred size and secure to inside of crown.

5 FINISHING

Weave in all ends to the back of the work. Soak beanie in cool water for 20 minutes to allow stitches to relax and bloom. Press dry between towels. Shape, using a hat blocker, or a balloon inflated to correct dimensions. Leave to fully dry.

Enjoy your Gradient Mesh beanie!

CHART

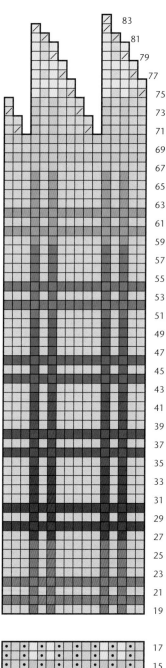

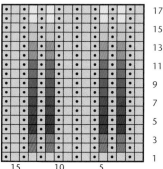

KEY

- ☐ A Birkin: k
- ▨ B Campion: k
- ■ C Gloamin': k
- ▨ D Lochan: k
- ▨ E Tarbet: k
- ▨ F Ardlui: k
- ▨ G Garth: k
- ☐ H Stockiemuir: k
- ☐ I Cowslip: k
- ⊡ p in shade indicated
- Ⓜ m1 in in shade indicated
- ▨ k2tog in shade indicated
- ☐ pattern repeat
- 18 increase round

COLOURWAY 1

COLOURWAY 2

GRADIENT MESH GAUNTLETS

Make yourself a matching set with the Gradient Mesh beanie!

YARN

Kate Davies Designs Milarrochy Tweed (70% Wool; 30% Mohair; 100m / 109yds per 25g ball)
1 ball of each of the following shades:

A Birkin   **F** Ardlui
B Campion   **G** Garth
C Gloamin'   **H** Stockiemuir
D Lochan   **I** Cowslip
E Tarbet

Size L requires additional ball of shade A.

NEEDLES AND NOTIONS

Gauge-size needle(s) of your preferred type for working small circumferences
Below gauge-size needle(s) of your preferred type for working small circumferences
Waste yarn (for holding thumb stitches)
Stitch markers
Tapestry needle

GAUGE

32 stitches and 36 rounds to 10cm / 4in over stranded colourwork in the round on gauge-size needle(s)
Use 3mm needle(s) as a starting point for swatching.

SIZES

S/M (M/L) to fit adult hand with 17-19cm / 6½-7½in (18-20.5cm / 7-8in) circumference

PATTERN NOTES

These gauntlets are worked from bottom to top. After the cuff, the hand is worked in stranded colourwork, with an integrated thumb gusset. Pay close attention to shade changes and purl stitches when working rib at cuff and top. Where one number is given, this applies to both sizes.

CHART NOTES

Read chart from right to left and repeat twice across each round.

INSTRUCTIONS

1
CAST ON, WORK CUFF

Using shade A (colourway 1) or shade B (colourway 2), below gauge-size needle(s), and long-tail cast on (or your preferred method) cast on 56 (64) sts, pm, and join for working in the round.
Rounds 1-25: Reading chart from right to left and changing shades where indicated, work in 1x1 rib as foll:
(K1, p1) around, paying close attention to the shade changes. Break off each shade when necessary, weaving in its tail on subsequent rounds.

2
WORK HAND

Rounds 26-44 (50): Change to gauge-size needle(s), and work rounds 26-44 (50).

3
WORK THUMB GUSSET

Round 45 (51): Insert thumb gusset as foll:
K28 (32) sts in pattern, pm, m1, pm, k28 (32) sts in pattern. *1 st inc; 57 (65) sts*
Following hand and gusset charts as est, working increases where indicated, work chart rounds 46-65 (52-71). *18 (18) sts inc; 75 (83) sts*
Round 66 (72): K28 (32), sl19 gusset sts to waste yarn, rm, k28 (32). *56 (64) sts rem*

4
COMPLETE HAND

Rounds 67-81 (73-89): Work hand from chart as est.

5
WORK TOP RIB

Rounds 82-89 (90-97): Change to below gauge-size needle(s), and work rib from chart as est paying close attention to the shade changes across the 1x1 rib pattern. Break off each shade when necessary, weaving in its tail on subsequent rounds.
Bind off in shade A (colourway 1) or shade B (colourway 2). Break yarn.

6
COMPLETE THUMB

Sl19 gusset stitches from waste yarn to below gauge-size needle(s) and work thumb as foll:

Size S/M only
Round 66: Puk1 st in the gap where thumb meets palm, work 19 sts from chart, pm, and join for working in the round. *20 sts*

Size M/L only
Round 72: Puk1 st in the gap where thumb meets palm, work 19 sts from chart, puk2 sts in the gap where thumb meets palm, pm, and join for working in the round. *22 sts*

Rounds 67-73 (73-79): Work rib from chart as est paying close attention to the shade changes across the 1x1 rib pattern. Bind off in shade A (colourway 1) or shade B (colourway 2).
Make a second gauntlet to match.

7
FINISHING

Weave in all ends to the back of the work, using yarn ends to carefully close any remaining gaps at the base of thumb. Soak gauntlets in cool water for 20 minutes to allow stitches to relax and bloom. Press dry between towels. Shape gauntlets using glove blockers (if you have them) or pins to position thumb. Dry flat, and leave to fully dry.

Enjoy your Gradient Mesh gauntlets!

SMALL/MEDIUM CHART
(shown in colourway 2)

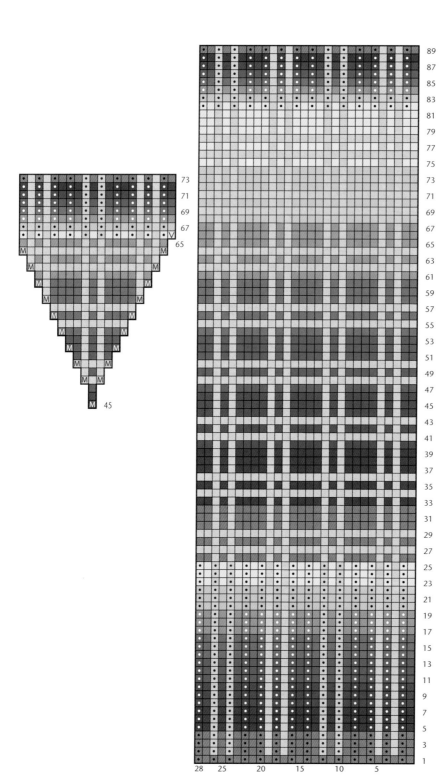

KEY

☐ A Birkin: k

▨ B Campion: k

■ C Gloamin': k

▨ D Lochan: k

▨ E Tarbet: k

▨ F Ardlui: k

▨ G Garth: k

☐ H Stockiemuir: k

☐ I Cowslip: k

• p in shade indicated

M m1 in in shade indicated

V puk1 in shade indicated

☐ pattern repeat

PATTERN REPEAT

MEDIUM/LARGE CHART
(shown in colourway 1)

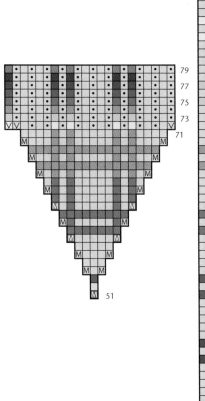

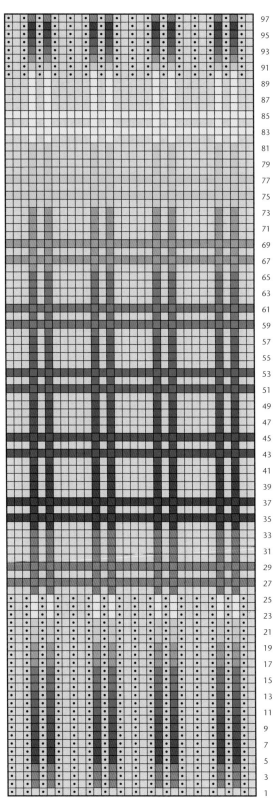

KEY

☐	A Birkin: k
▨	B Campion: k
▨	C Gloamin': k
▨	D Lochan: k
▨	E Tarbet: k
▨	F Ardlui: k
▨	G Garth: k
☐	H Stockiemuir: k
☐	I Cowslip: k
•	p in shade indicated
M	m1 in in shade indicated
V	puk1 in shade indicated
☐	pattern repeat

PATTERN REPEAT

E L E C T R I C
U P S & D O W N S

Fun, flip-top fingerless gloves / mittens, in gradient shades, featuring a motif reminiscent of woven fabrics and a decorative, woven button.

ELECTRIC UPS & DOWNS

YARN

Kate Davies Designs Milarrochy Tweed (70% Wool; 30% Mohair; 100m / 109yds per 25g ball)

1 ball of each of the following shades:

Size S	Size L
A Birkin	**A** Birkin
B Smirr	**B** Tarbet
C Ardlui	**C** Gloamin'
D Tarbet	**D** Cranachan
E Gloamin'	**E** Campion

Other possible colourways are shown in accompanying swatches. This is a great pattern for experimenting with colour.

NEEDLES AND NOTIONS

Gauge-size needle(s) of your preferred type for working small circumferences
Below gauge-size needle(s) of your preferred type for working small circumferences
Gauge-size needle(s) of your preferred type for working fingers
Gauge-size dpns or short circular needle for working i-cord
Long gauge-size circular needles (or holder) for holding finger stitches
Waste yarn (for holding thumb stitches)
Stitch markers
Tapestry needle

GAUGE

32 stitches and 36 rounds to 10cm / 4in over stranded stockinette in the round on gauge-size needle(s)
Use 3mm needle(s) as a starting point for swatching.

SIZES

S (L) to fit adult hand with 17-19cm / 6½ -7½ in (21-2cm / 8-9in) circumference

PATTERN NOTES

These mittens are worked from bottom to top. After the corrugated rib cuff, the hand is worked in stranded colourwork with stitches inserted for an afterthought thumb. Fingers and thumb are completed, before finishing the flip-top, continuing the colourwork seamlessly. The mitten top is finished with an i-cord loop and attached with a simple-to-make woven button.

SPECIAL TECHNIQUES

i-cord

Work on dpns or short circular needle:
K3, slide sts to opposite end of needle, pull working yarn across the back; repeat from * for desired length.

Covered button

Follow the instructions in this tutorial:
https://kddandco.com/2014/02/20/covered-button-tutorial/

CHART NOTES

Read chart from right to left and repeat chart 1 twice across each round, taking note of oppositional thumb placement for left and right hand. Chart 2 shows both sides of the flip-top and is repeated once. Note that unused shades are carried and caught across the back of the work when beginning the flip-top rib.

INSTRUCTIONS

1 CAST ON, WORK CUFF

With shade C, below gauge-size needle(s), and using the long-tail cast on (or your preferred method) cast on 56 (64) sts, pm, and join for working in the round.
Chart round 1: K.
Rounds 2-16 (2-18): Changing shades as indicated, work 1x1 twisted rib as foll:
(K1tbl A, p1C) around.
Break C and weave in tail on next round.

2 WORK HAND

Rounds 17-41 (19-45): Change to gauge-size needle(s) and, changing shades as indicated, work chart rounds 17-41 (19-45).

3 PLACE THUMB

Right Hand
Round 42 (46): K1 in pattern, k9 (10) with waste yarn, return last 9 (10) sts to lh needle, then, with working yarn, work across these sts in pattern, and complete round as est.

Left Hand
Round 42 (46): K18 (21) in pattern, k9 (10) with waste yarn, return last 9 (10) sts to lh needle, then, with working yarn, work across these sts in pattern, and complete round as est.

4 COMPLETE HAND; PLACE FLIP-TOP

Work rounds 43-60 (47-62) from chart 1 as est.
Round 61 (63): K28 (32) in pattern, kfb28 (32) in pattern. *28 (32) sts inc; 84 (96) sts*
Moving sts around needle without knitting, sl each alternate stitch from back of hand to waste yarn. *56 (64) hand sts and 28 (32) flip-top sts set aside*
Complete rounds 62-68 (64-74) from chart as est.

5 HALF FINGERS

Right Hand
Index Finger
With A and gauge-size needle(s), work index finger as foll:

Round 1: K8 (9) sts, using backward-loop cast on, cast on 2 (2) sts in the gap between fingers, sl20 (23) sts to holder or spare needle (palm), sl20 (23) sts to a second holder (back of hand), k8 (9), pm, and join for working in the round. *18 (20) sts*
Rounds 2-9: K.
Round 10 (12): Bind off. Break yarn.

Middle Finger
With A and gauge-size needle(s), work middle finger as foll:
Round 1: Sl7 (8) sts from palm sts holder, k7 (8), using backward-loop cast on, cast on 1 (1) st in the gap between fingers, sl7 (8) sts from back of hand sts holder, k7 (8), using backward-loop cast on, cast on 1 (1) st in the gap between fingers, pm, and join for working in the round. *16 (18) sts*
Rounds 2-9 (2-11): K16 (18).
Round 10 (12): Bind off. Break yarn.

Ring Finger
With A and gauge-size needle(s), work ring finger as foll:
Round 1: Sl7 (8) sts from palm sts holder, k7 (8), using backward-loop cast on, cast on 1 (1) st in the gap between fingers, sl7 (8) sts from back of hand sts holder, k7 (8), using backward-loop cast on, cast on 1 (1) st in the gap between fingers, pm, and join for working in the round. *16 (18) sts*
Rounds 2-9 (2-11): K16 (18).
Round 10 (12): Bind off. Break yarn.

Little Finger
With A and gauge-size needle(s), work little fingers as foll:
Round 1: Sl the last 6 (7) sts from palm sts holder, k6 (7), sl the last 6 (7) sts from back of hand sts holder, k6 (7), using backward-loop cast on, cast on 1 (2) sts in the gap between fingers, pm, and join for working in the round. *13 (16) sts*
Rounds 2-9 (2-11): K13 (16).
Round 10 (12): Bind off. Break yarn.

Left Hand
Little Finger
With A and gauge-size needle(s), work little finger as foll:
Round 1: K6 (7), using backward-loop cast on, cast on 1(2) sts in the gap between fingers, sl22 (25) sts to holder or spare needle (palm), sl22 (25) sts to a second holder (back of hand), k6

(7), pm, and join for working in the round. *13 (16) sts*
Rounds 2-9 (2-11): K13 (16).
Round 10 (12): Bind off. Break yarn.

Ring Finger

With A and gauge-size needle(s), work ring finger as foll:
Round 1: Sl7 (8) sts from palm sts holder, k7 (8), using backward-loop cast on, cast on 1 (1) st in the gap between fingers, sl7 (8) sts from back of hand sts holder, k7 (8), using backward-loop cast on, cast on 1 (1) st in the gap between fingers, pm, and join for working in the round. *16 (18) sts*
Rounds 2-9 (2-11): K16 (18).
Round 10 (12): Bind off. Break yarn.

Middle Finger

With A and gauge-size needle(s), work middle finger as foll:
Round 1: Sl7 (8) sts from palm sts holder, k7 (8), using backward-loop cast on, cast on 1 (1) st in the gap between fingers, sl7 (8) sts from back of hand sts holder, k7 (8), using backward-loop cast on, cast on 1 (1) st in the gap between fingers, pm, and join for working in the round. *16 (18) sts*
Rounds 2-9 (2-11): K16 (18).
Round 10 (12): Bind off. Break yarn.

Index Finger

With A and gauge-size needle(s), work index finger as foll:
Round 1: Sl the last 8 (9) sts from palm sts holder, k8 (9), sl the last 8 (9) sts from back of hand sts holder, k8 (9), using backward-loop cast on, cast on 2 (2) sts in the gap between fingers, pm, and join for working in the round. *18 (20) sts*
Rounds 2-9 (2-11): K18 (20).
Round 10 (12): Bind off. Break yarn.

6 WORK THUMB

Carefully remove waste yarn and sl18 (20) sts to gauge-size needle(s).
Round 1: With A, *k9 (10), puk1 (2) in the gap where thumb meets palm*, repeat from * once, pm, and join for working in the round. *20 (24) sts*
Rounds 2-22 (2-27): K20 (24).
Round 23 (28): (K2tog) around. *10 (12) sts dec; 10 (12) sts rem*
Round 24 (29): (K2tog) around. *5 (6) sts dec; 5*

(6) sts rem
Break yarn. Draw yarn up through remaining 5 (6) sts, draw down through centre and fasten off to WS of work.

7 WORK FLIP-TOP

With gauge-size needle(s), work flip-top from chart 2 as foll:
Round 62 (64): With C (small) or A (large) and gauge-size needle(s), cast on 28 (32) sts, sl28 (32) sts from waste yarn to gauge-size working needles, k28 (32) in pattern. *56 (64) sts*
Rounds 63-67 (65-70): Work 1x1 twisted rib across first 28 (32) sts, completing the rest of the round in pattern, joining in, carrying and catching 2 shades unused for first half of round across the back of the work.
Rounds 68-89 (71-95): Complete flip-top, working decreases as indicated. *36 (40) sts dec; 20 (24) sts rem*
Graft together 2 sets of 10 (12) sts. Break yarn.

Make a second mitt to match.

8 LOOP (MAKE 2)

With shade E, below gauge-size needle(s), cast on 3 sts. Work in i-cord for 28 rows or until the length is 6.5cm / 2½in.

9 COVERED BUTTON

Choose a button of 1.2cm / ½in in diameter and following the linked tutorial, weave a button cover in your preferred shades (illustrated here in shades C, D and E). If you prefer a plain button, choose one with 2.5cm / 1in diameter.

10 FINISHING

Weave in all ends to the back of the work, using yarn ends to carefully close any remaining gaps at the base of fingers and thumb. Fix each loop at the top of the flip-top. Soak gloves in cool water for 20 minutes to allow stitches to relax and bloom. Press dry between towels. Shape gloves using glove blockers (if you have them) or pins to position thumb and fingers. Dry flat, and leave to fully dry.

Enjoy your Electric Ups & Downs!

COLOUR MOVES

SMALL CHART 1

LARGE CHART 1

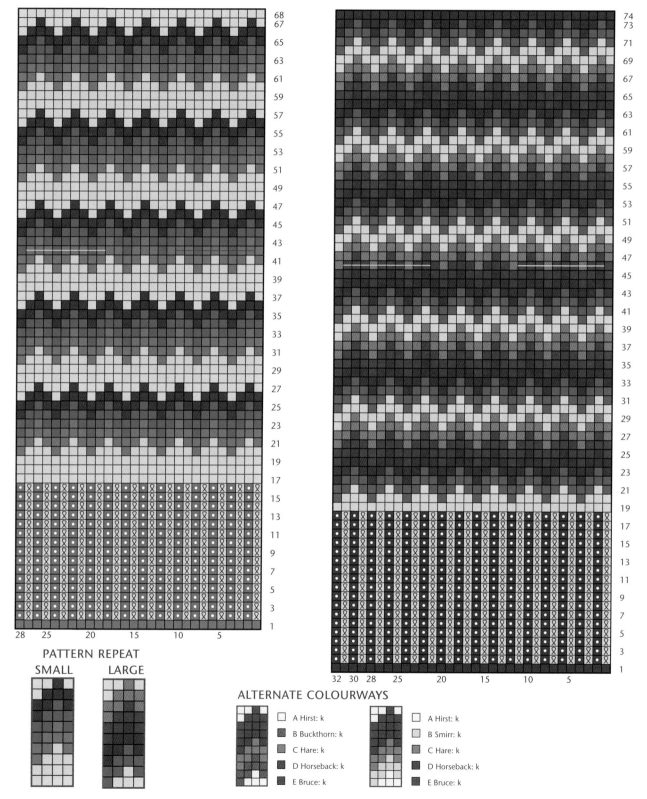

PATTERN REPEAT
SMALL LARGE

ALTERNATE COLOURWAYS

	A Hirst: k			A Hirst: k
	B Buckthorn: k			B Smirr: k
	C Hare: k			C Hare: k
	D Horseback: k			D Horseback: k
	E Bruce: k			E Bruce: k

SMALL CHART 2

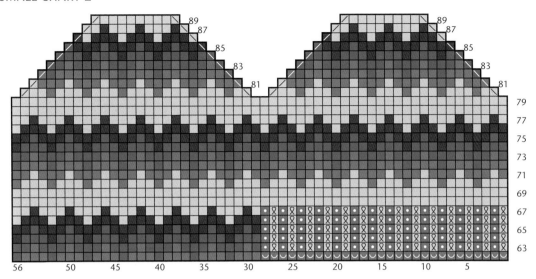

LARGE CHART 2

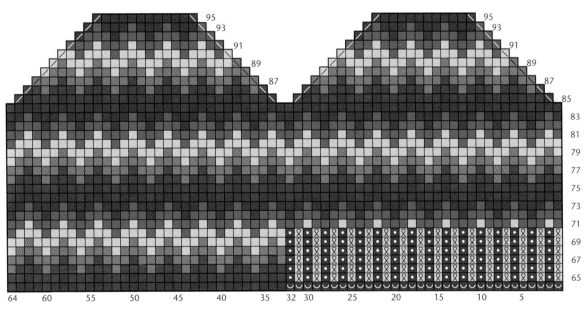

KEY (SMALL)

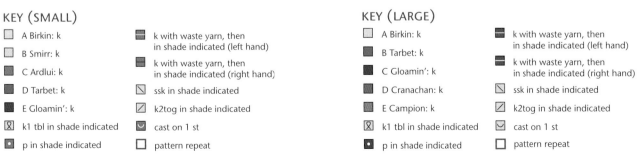

☐ A Birkin: k	▬ k with waste yarn, then in shade indicated (left hand)
☐ B Smirr: k	▬ k with waste yarn, then in shade indicated (right hand)
☐ C Ardlui: k	◊ ssk in shade indicated
☐ D Tarbet: k	◊ k2tog in shade indicated
☐ E Gloamin': k	◡ cast on 1 st
⊠ k1 tbl in shade indicated	☐ pattern repeat
⊡ p in shade indicated	

KEY (LARGE)

☐ A Birkin: k	▬ k with waste yarn, then in shade indicated (left hand)
☐ B Tarbet: k	▬ k with waste yarn, then in shade indicated (right hand)
☐ C Gloamin': k	◊ ssk in shade indicated
☐ D Cranachan: k	◊ k2tog in shade indicated
☐ E Campion: k	◡ cast on 1 st
⊠ k1 tbl in shade indicated	☐ pattern repeat
⊡ p in shade indicated	

51

SIRENTE

This design was inspired by textiles and carpets I admired during my travels in Peru. As well as finding Peruvian designs and patterns incredibly inspiring, I feel a deep personal sense of connection to its rocky, mountain landscape, which reminds me of my Abruzzo birthplace, and its characteristic peaks, such as Sirente, from which this design takes its name.

SIRENTE

YARN

Kate Davies Designs Milarrochy Tweed (70% Wool; 30% Mohair; 100m / 109yds per 25g ball)

A Hirst: 2 x 25g balls
B Cranachan: 1 x 25 g ball
C Gloamin': 1 x 25 g ball
D Garth: 1 x 25 g ball
(Alternate colourways are suggested in accompanying swatches.)

NEEDLES AND NOTIONS

Gauge-size needle(s) of your preferred type for working small circumferences
Below gauge-size needle(s) of your preferred type for working small circumferences
Waste yarn (for holding thumb stitches)
Stitch markers
Tapestry needle

GAUGE

32 stitches and 36 rounds to 10cm / 4in over stranded stockinette in the round on gauge-size needle(s)
Use 3mm needle(s) as a starting point for swatching.

SIZE

This pattern creates a fairly large fitting pair of mittens, to fit hand with 21-22cm / 8-9in circumference. They can be comfortably worn, as shown, by smaller hands over a hand-knitted lining or another pair of mitts or gloves, to create a cosy outer layer.

PATTERN NOTES

These mittens are worked from bottom to top. After the corrugated rib cuff, the hand is worked in stranded colourwork, with an integrated thumb gusset. The thumb top is completed at the end.

CHART NOTES

Due to the odd number of repeats, and in order to create two mirroring gloves the pattern has two charts: for left and right hands. Read from right to left throughout.

INSTRUCTIONS

1 CAST ON, WORK CUFF

With shade A, below gauge-size needle(s), and using long-tail cast on (or your preferred method), cast on 66 sts, pm, and join for working in the round.
Rounds 1-19: Reading chart from right to left, changing shades where indicated, and weaving in yarn ends on subsequent rounds, work cuff in 2x1 twisted rib: [(k1tbl twice), p1] around.

2 WORK HAND

Change to gauge-size needle(s), and changing shades where indicated, begin working from chart for relevant hand.
Note: Try keeping shades A & C 'live' throughout, carrying both yarns up the back of the work, and breaking off and weaving in shades B & D as you go.
Work chart rounds 20-36.

3 WORK THUMB GUSSET

Round 37: K33 in pattern, pm, m1, pm, k33 in pattern. *1 st inc; 67 sts*
Rounds 38-57: Work from hand and thumb gusset charts as est. *18 sts inc; 85 sts*
Round 58: K33, rm, slip 19 gusset sts to waste yarn or holder, rm, k33. *66 sts rem*

4 COMPLETE HAND AND MITTEN TOP

Rounds 59-97: Complete hand charts as est, working decreases as indicated.
44 sts dec; 22 sts rem
With A graft together 2 sets of 11 sts.

5 COMPLETE THUMB

Sl19 gusset sts from waste yarn to gauge-size needles.

Right thumb
Round 58: Puk2 sts in the gap where thumb meets palm, k19, puk1 st in the gap, pm, and join for working in the round. *22 sts*

Left thumb
Round 58: Puk1 st in the gap where thumb meets palm, k19, puk2 sts in the gap, pm, and join for working in the round. *22 sts*

Both thumbs
Rounds 59-79: Work as est from thumb chart, decreasing as indicated. *17 sts dec; 5 sts rem*
Break yarn. Draw yarn up through remaining 5 stitches, draw down through centre, and fasten off to WS of work.

Make a second mitten to match.

6 FINISHING

Weave in all ends to the back of the work, using yarn ends to carefully close any remaining gaps at the thumb base. Soak mittens in cool water for 20 minutes to allow stitches to relax and bloom. Press dry between towels. Shape mittens using glove blockers (if you have them) or pins to position thumb. Dry flat, and leave to fully dry.

Enjoy your Sirente mittens!

LEFT HAND CHART

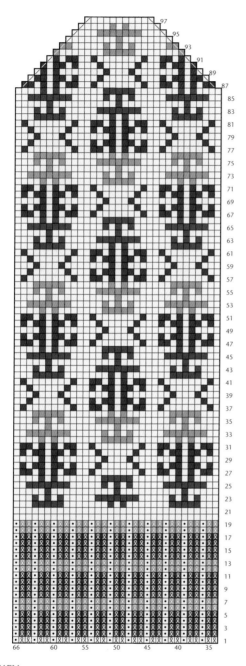

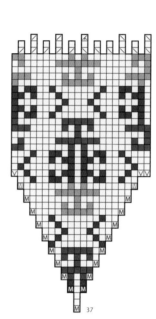

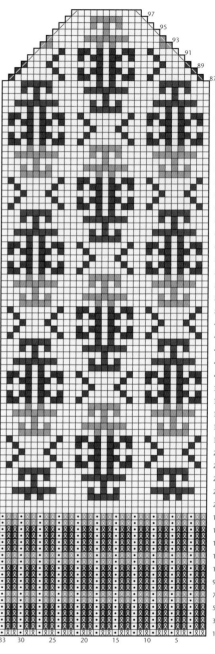

KEY

<table>
<tr><td>□</td><td>A Hirst: k</td><td>⊘</td><td>k2tog in shade indicated</td></tr>
<tr><td>■</td><td>B Cranachan: k</td><td>⊠</td><td>k3tog in shade indicated</td></tr>
<tr><td>■</td><td>C Gloamin': k</td><td>M</td><td>m1 in in shade indicated</td></tr>
<tr><td>▦</td><td>D Garth: k</td><td>Ⅴ</td><td>puk1 in shade indicated</td></tr>
<tr><td>Ⓡ</td><td>k1 tbl in shade indicated</td><td>□</td><td>pattern repeat</td></tr>
<tr><td>·</td><td>p in shade indicated</td><td></td><td></td></tr>
<tr><td>◩</td><td>ssk in shade indicated</td><td></td><td></td></tr>
</table>

PATTERN REPEAT

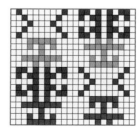

ALTERNATIVE SWATCH

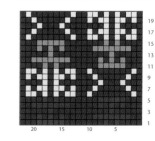

A Gloamin
B Cranach
C Cowslip.
D Garth: k
pattern re

RIGHT HAND CHART

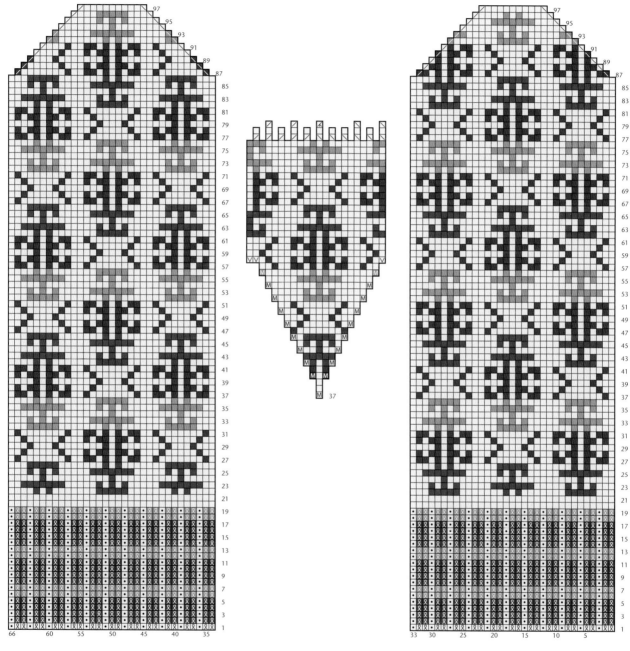

ALTERNATIVE SWATCHES

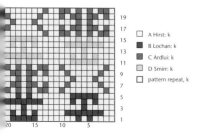

☐ A Hirst: k
■ B Lochan: k
▨ C Ardlui: k
☐ D Smirr: k
☐ pattern repeat, k

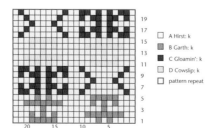

☐ A Hirst: k
▨ B Garth: k
■ C Gloamin': k
▨ D Cowslip: k
☐ pattern repeat

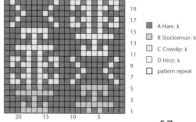

■ A Hare: k
▨ B Stockiemuir: k
☐ C Cowslip: k
☐ D Hirst: k
☐ pattern repeat

GRAN SASSO

Gran Sasso, which means Big Stone, is a majestic and fascinating mountain - the highest in the Italian Appennines, standing at 2,912m. The dusky shades of this pair of designs are reminiscent of those of Gran Sasso on a soft, autumnal evening, while the corrugated texture shared by both hat and mittens is evocative of this rugged, and rewarding mountain.

GRAN SASSO SLOUCH

YARN

Kate Davies Designs Àrd Thìr (60% Peruvian Highland Wool; 40% Alpaca; 65m / 71yds per 50g skein)
A Firemore: 2 x 50g skeins
B Kintra: 2 x 50g skeins

NEEDLES AND NOTIONS

Gauge-size needle(s) of your preferred type for working in the round
Gauge-size needle(s) of your preferred type for working small circumferences
Below gauge-size needle(s) of your preferred type for working in the round
Gauge-size dpns or short circular needle for working i-cord
Stitch markers (x8, for marking i-cord)
Tapestry needle

GAUGE

22 stitches and 26 rounds to 10cm / 4in over pattern in the round on gauge-size needle(s)
Use 4.5mm needle(s) as a starting point for swatching.

SIZE

To fit adult head with 51-56cm / 20-22in circumference
This hat is quite roomy, so should accommodate most adult sizes.

SPECIAL TECHNIQUES

m1p: Make 1 stitch purlwise. The following tutorial may be useful: https://www.youtube.com/watch?v=rIlBu_3-lzM

i-cord

Work on dpns or short circular needle:
K3, slide sts to opposite end of needle, pull working yarn across the back; repeat from * for desired length.

PATTERN NOTES

This hat is worked from bottom to top in two shades which are worked on alternate rounds. The crown is finished with decorative i-cord loops.

INSTRUCTIONS

1 CAST ON, WORK BRIM

With shade A, below gauge-size needle(s), and using long-tail cast on (or your preferred method), cast on 93 sts, pm, and join for working in the round.
Round 1: With shade A, (k2, p1) around.
Round 2: With B, (k2, p1) around.
Repeat rounds 1 and 2 3 more times. *8 rounds worked*

2 WORK HAT BODY

Change to gauge-size needle(s) and, on next round, increase as foll:
Round 9: With A, (k1, m1p, p2) around. *31 sts inc; 124 sts*
Rounds 10-49: Continuing to change shades on alternating rounds as est, (k1, p3) around.

3 WORK CROWN

Round 50: (K1, p2tog, p1) around. *31 sts dec; 93 sts rem*
Round 51: (K1, p2) around.
Round 52: (K1, p2tog) around (shift to smaller needles as necessary). *31 sts dec; 62 sts rem*
Round 53: (K1, p1) around.
Round 54: (K2tog) around. *31 sts dec; 31 sts rem*
Round 55: K31.
Round 56: K1, *k2tog; repeat from * to end of round. *15 sts dec; 16 sts rem*
Round 57: (K2tog) around. *8 sts dec; 8 sts rem*
Break yarn. Draw yarn up through remaining 8 sts, draw down through centre and fasten off to WS of work.

4 I-CORD LOOPS

With shade B, and below gauge-size needle(s) cast on 3 sts.
*Knit 28 rows in i-cord, pm; repeat from * 8 times. Bind off leaving a 30cm / 11¾in tail. Sew the i-cord to the centre top of the hat, first stitching down the cast-on edge, then anchoring and stitching the points marked by each of the markers, removing the markers as you go. Finally, stitch down the bound-off edge. There will be 9 loops in total. Stitch down securely, and fasten off to WS of work.

5 FINISHING

Weave in all ends to the back of the work. Soak hat in cool water for 20 minutes to allow stitches to relax and bloom. Press dry between towels. Shape hat, using a hat blocker or a balloon (inflated to fit). Leave to fully dry.

Enjoy your Gran Sasso slouch!

GRAN SASSO MITTENS

Make yourself a matching set with the Gran Sasso slouch!

YARN

Kate Davies Designs Àrd Thìr (60% Peruvian Highland Wool; 40% Alpaca; 65m / 71yds per 50g skein)
A Firemore: 2 x 50g skeins
B Kintra: 2 x 50g skeins

NEEDLES AND NOTIONS

Gauge-size needle(s) of your preferred type for working small circumferences
Below gauge-size needle(s) of your preferred type for working small circumferences
Waste yarn (for holding thumb stitches)
Stitch markers
Tapestry needle

GAUGE

22 stitches and 26 rounds to 10cm / 4in over pattern in the round on gauge-size needle(s)
Use 4.5mm needle(s) as a starting point for swatching.

SIZE

To fit adult hand with 18-20.5cm / 7-8in circumference

PATTERN NOTES

These mittens are worked from bottom to top, following a simple striped pattern in alternating shades, with an afterthought thumb.

INSTRUCTIONS

1 CAST ON, WORK CUFF

Using shade A, below gauge-size needle(s), and using long-tail cast on (or your preferred method), cast on 36 sts, pm, and join for working in the round.
Round 1: With shade A, (k2, p1) around.
Round 2: With B, (k2, p1) around.
Repeat rounds 1 and 2 6 more times. *14 rounds worked*

2 WORK HAND

Change to gauge-size needle(s), and work hand as foll:
Rounds 15-30: Continuing to change shades on alternate rounds as est, (k1, p3) around.

3 PLACE THUMB

Right hand
Round 31: K1, with waste yarn, work next 5 sts, return last 5 sts to lh needle, then, work across these sts with working yarn in pattern, and complete round in pattern as est.

Left hand
Round 31: (K1, p3) 4 times, with waste yarn, work next 5 sts, return last 5 sts to lh needle, then, with working yarn, work across these sts in pattern, and complete round as est.

4 WORK MITTEN TOP

Rounds 32-46: (K1, p3) around.
Round 47: (K1, p2tog, p1) around. *9 sts dec; 27 sts rem*
Round 48: (K1, p2tog) around. *9 sts dec; 18 sts rem*
Round 49: (K2tog) around. *9 sts dec; 9 sts rem*
Break yarn. Draw up through remaining 9 sts, draw down through centre and fasten off to WS of work

5 COMPLETE THUMB

Carefully remove waste yarn and sl10 sts to gauge-size needle(s).
Round 1: With A, *k5, puk1 in the gap where thumb meets palm*, repeat from * once, pm, and join for working in the round. *12 sts*
Rounds 2-12: (K1, p3) around.
Round 13: (K1, p2tog, p1) around. *3 sts dec; 9 sts rem*
Round 14: (K1, p2tog) around. *3 sts dec; 6 sts rem*
Break yarn. Draw up through remaining 6 sts, draw down through centre and fasten off to WS of work.

Make a second mitten to match.

6 FINISHING

Weave in all ends to the back of the work, using yarn ends to carefully close any remaining gaps at thumb base. Soak mittens in cool water for 20 minutes to allow stitches to relax and bloom. Press dry between towels. Shape mittens using glove blockers (if you have them) or pins to position thumb. Dry flat, and leave to fully dry.

Enjoy your Gran Sasso mittens!

TAIGHEAN

This pattern is based around a simple house motif and uses 7 shade combinations. Each row of houses is a different shade, following a gradient, offset by a half motif from each previous row of houses. This design recalls colours I've enjoyed during my trips to Scotland: it was the first pattern I designed for Kate and since then I can't seem to stop designing gloves and mittens!
'Taighean' means 'houses' in Scottish Gaelic.

TAIGHEAN

YARN

Kate Davies Designs Milarrochy Tweed (70% Wool; 30% Mohair; 100m / 109yds per 25g ball)
1 ball of each of the following shades:
A Gloamin'
B Birkin
C Smirr
D Tarbet
E Ardlui
F Garth
G Stockiemuir

NEEDLES AND NOTIONS

Gauge-size needle(s) of your preferred type for working small circumferences
Below gauge-size needle(s) of your preferred type for working small circumferences
Waste yarn (for holding thumb stitches)
Stitch markers
Tapestry needle

GAUGE

32 stitches and 36 rounds to 10cm / 4in over stranded colourwork in the round on gauge-size needle(s)
Use 3mm needle(s) as a starting point for swatching.

SIZE

To fit adult hand with 17-19cm / 6½-7½in circumference

PATTERN NOTES

These mitts are worked from bottom to top. After the long corrugated rib cuff, the hand is worked in stranded colourwork, with an incorporated thumb gusset. Corrugated rib (whose length can be extended, if a longer mitt is required) completes the top. The thumb top is similarly finished in corrugated rib.

CHART NOTES

This pattern has two charts for the left and right hands (to create a mirroring pattern), each of which includes cuff, thumb gusset, palm and back of hand. Ensure you are working from the correct hand chart, and read the charts from right to left throughout.

INSTRUCTIONS

1 CAST ON, WORK CUFF

With shade A, below gauge-size needle(s), and using a long-tail cast on (or your preferred method), cast on 56 sts, pm, and join for working in the round.

Rounds 1 & 2: Reading chart from right to left, k56. Break A and weave in tail on next round.

Round 3: Join in B and (k2, p2) around (2x2 rib).

Rounds 4 - 23: Changing shades and working purl sts as indicated, and weaving in tails after each shade change on subsequent rounds, work chart rounds 4-23.

2 WORK HAND

Change to gauge-size needle(s), and, working chart from right to left and changing shades as indicated, begin working from chart round 24, following correct chart for left or right hand. Work chart rounds 25-36.

3 WORK THUMB GUSSET

Reading charts from right to left, insert thumb gusset chart as foll:

Round 37: K28 sts in pattern, pm, m1, pm, k28 in pattern. *1 st inc; 57 sts*

Rounds 38- 56: Work from charts as est, increasing where indicated. *17 sts inc; 73 sts*

Round 57: K28, rm, slip 17 gusset sts to waste yarn, rm, k28. *56 sts rem*

4 COMPLETE HAND

Rounds 58-64: K56 in pattern. Break A.

Round 65: With B, k56.

5 WORK TOP RIB

Change to below gauge-size needle(s), and, working purl sts and changing shades as indicated, begin working corrugated rib from chart round 66.

Work chart rounds 67-70.

Round 71: With B, (k2, p2) around. Break B.

Round 72: Join in A, (k2, p2) around, and bind off.

6 COMPLETE THUMB

Slip 17 thumb gusset stitches from waste yarn to below gauge-size needle(s). With B work thumb as foll:

Left thumb

Round 65: Puk1 st in the gap where thumb meets palm, k17, puk2 sts in the gap, pm, and join for working in the round. *20 sts*

Right thumb

Round 65: Puk2 sts in the gap where thumb meets palm, k17, puk1 st in the gap, pm, and join for working in the round. *20 sts*

Both thumbs

Working purl sts and changing shades as indicated, begin working corrugated rib from chart rounds 58-63.

Round 64: With B, (k2, p2) around. Break B.

Round 65: Join in A, (k2, p2) around and bind off.

Make a second mitt to match.

7 FINISHING

Weave in all ends to the back of the work, using yarn ends to carefully close any remaining gaps at thumb base. Soak mitts in cool water for 20 minutes to allow stitches to relax and bloom. Press dry between towels. Shape mitts using glove blockers (if you have them) or pins to position thumb. Dry flat, and leave to fully dry.

Enjoy your Taighean mitts!

LEFT HAND CHART

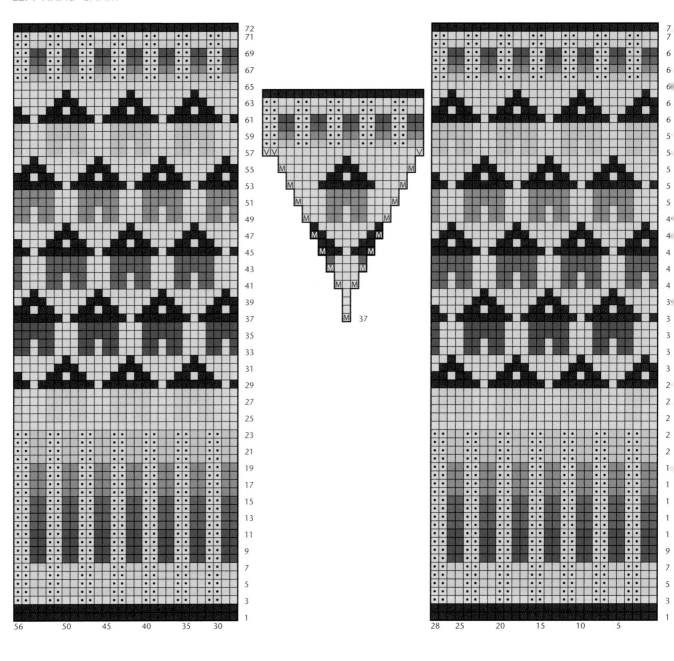

KEY

■ A Gloamin': k	▣ p in shade indicated
□ B Birkin: k	Ⓜ m1 in in shade indicated
□ C Smirr: k	Ⓥ puk1 in shade indicated
■ D Tarbet: k	□ pattern repeat
■ E Ardlui: k	
■ F Garth: k	
□ G Stockiemuir: k	

RIGHT HAND CHART

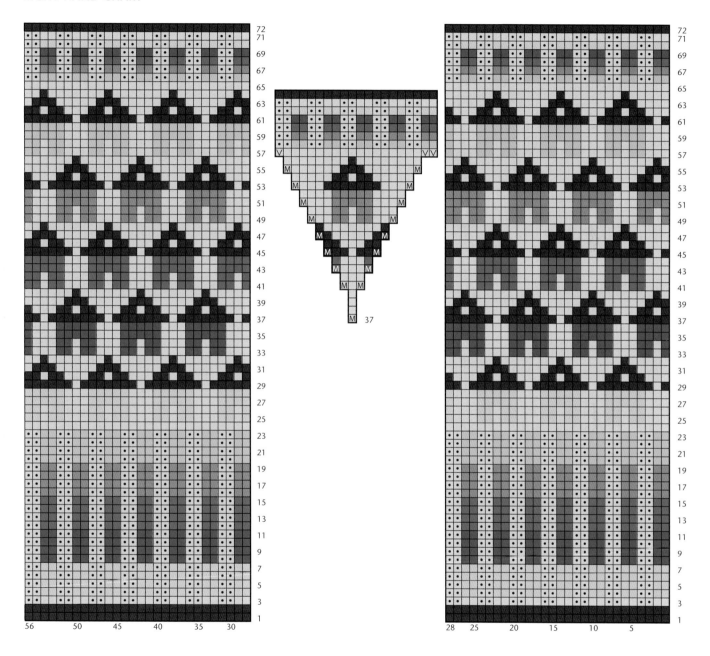

PATTERN REPEAT

FLORAL
TAPESTRY

This design was inspired by one of the sketches I drew during my travels to Peru in 2014. It is based on a flower with 4 petals in a pattern with 4 complimentary shades. Each repeat of the flower is worked in a different shade, half-shifted from the previous repeat, with a dotted motif in another bold shade inbetween. When knitted up, the final result reminded me of a carpet, with the cuff playing the framing role of the carpet border.

FLORAL TAPESTRY TAM

YARN

Kate Davies Designs Milarrochy Tweed (70% Wool; 30% Mohair; 100m / 109yds per 25g ball)
1 ball of each of the following shades:
A Buckthorn
B Tarbet
C Garth
D Smirr

NEEDLES AND NOTIONS

Gauge-size needle(s) of your preferred type for working in the round
Below gauge-size needle(s) of your preferred type for working in the round
Stitch markers
Tapestry needle

GAUGE

32 stitches and 36 rounds to 10cm / 4in over stranded stockinette in the round on gauge-size needle(s)
Use 3mm needle(s) as a starting point for swatching.

SIZE

To fit adult head with 51-53.5cm / 20-21in circumference

PATTERN NOTES

This tam is worked from bottom to top. After the brim, the tam body is worked in stranded colourwork. This tam fits neatly, with a deeper length designed to cover the ears.

CHART NOTES

Read from right to left, repeating chart 6 times across each round.

INSTRUCTIONS

1

CAST ON, WORK BRIM

Using shade A, below gauge needle(s), and using long-tail cast on (or your preferred method) cast on 120 sts, pm, and join for working in the round.
Rounds 1-13: Reading chart from right to left and changing shades where indicated, work in 1x1 twisted rib:
(K1tbl, p1) around.

2

WORK TAM BODY

Change to gauge-size needle(s) and with A work increases as foll:
Round 14: (Kfb, k4) around. *24 sts inc; 144 sts*
Rounds 15-62: Work from chart.

3

WORK CROWN

Rounds 63-85: Shifting to shorter needle(s) as crown circumference reduces, follow chart, working decreases as indicated. *138 sts dec; 6 sts rem*
Break yarn. Draw yarn up through remaining 6 sts, draw down through centre and fasten off to WS of work.

4

FINISHING

Weave in all ends to the back of the work. Soak tam in cool water for 20 minutes to allow stitches to relax and bloom. Press dry between towels. Shape tam using a shallow dish with 19.5cm / 7¾ in diameter and leave to fully dry.

Enjoy your Floral Tapestry tam!

CHART

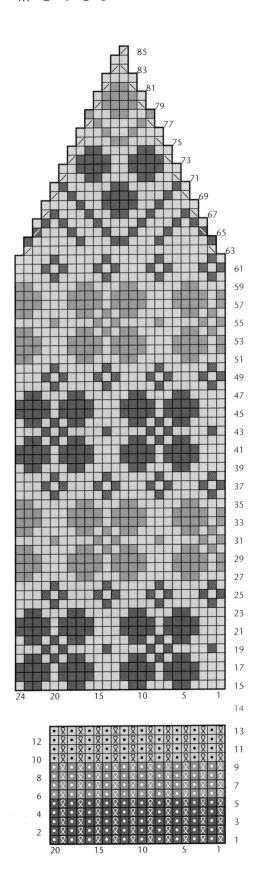

KEY

■ A Buckthorn: k

■ B Tarbet: k

■ C Garth: k

□ A Smirr: k

⟨ k1 tbl in shade indicated

• p in shade indicated

⟍ ssk in shade indicated

⟋ k2tog in shade indicated

□ pattern repeat

14 increase round

PATTERN REPEAT

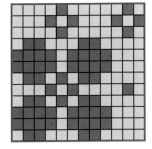

FLORAL TAPESTRY MITTENS

Make yourself a matching set with the Floral Tapestry tam!

YARN

Kate Davies Designs Milarrochy Tweed (70% Wool; 30% Mohair; 100m / 109yds per 25g ball)
1 ball of each of the following shades:
A Buckthorn
B Tarbet
C Garth
D Smirr

NEEDLES AND NOTIONS

Gauge-size needle(s) of your preferred type for working small circumferences
Below gauge-size needle(s) of your preferred type for working small circumferences
Waste yarn (for holding thumb stitches)
Stitch markers
Tapestry needle

GAUGE

32 stitches and 36 rounds to 10cm / 4in over stranded colourwork in the round on gauge-size needle(s)
Use 3mm needle(s) as a starting point for swatching.

SIZE

To fit adult hand with 18-20.5 cm / 7-8in circumference

PATTERN NOTES

These mittens are worked from bottom to top. After the 1x1 twisted rib cuff, the hand is worked in stranded colourwork, with an integrated thumb gusset.

SPECIAL TECHNIQUES

Tubular cast on
The following tutorial may be useful:
http://dyedreams.blogspot.com/2009/03/tubular-cast-on-in-round-for-socks.html

CHART NOTES

Read from right to left throughout. To create a pair of perfectly mirroring mittens across an odd number of repeats, this pattern has separate charts for left and right hands.

INSTRUCTIONS

1 CAST ON, WORK CUFF

Using shade A, below gauge needle(s), and using 1x1 long-tail tubular cast on (or your preferred method), cast on 60 sts, pm, and join for working in the round.
Rounds 1-20: Reading chart from right to left and changing shades as indicated, work chart rounds 1-20 in 1x1 twisted rib (k1tbl, p1) around.

2 WORK HAND

Rounds 21-36: Change to gauge-size needle(s), and ensuring you are working from the correct hand chart, work rounds 21-36, breaking off shades A, B and C in turn, and carrying shade D throughout.

3 WORK THUMB GUSSET

Place thumb gusset chart as foll:
Round 37: K30 in pattern, pm, m1, pm, k30 in pattern. *1 st inc; 61 sts*
Rounds 38-57: Work from charts as est. *18 sts inc; 79 sts*
Round 58: K30, rm, slip 19 gusset sts to waste yarn, rm, k30. *60 sts rem*

4 COMPLETE HAND

Rounds 59-83: K in pattern, following chart.

5 WORK MITTEN TOP

Rounds 84-93: Follow chart, working decreases as indicated. *40 sts dec; 20 sts rem*
With D graft together 2 sets of 10 sts.

6 COMPLETE THUMB

Sl19 gusset sts from waste yarn to gauge-size working needles and with D and C work thumb as foll:

Right thumb
Round 58: Puk2 sts in the gap where thumb meets palm, k19, puk1 st in the gap, pm, and join for working in the round. *22 sts*

Left thumb
Round 58: Puk1 st in the gap where thumb meets palm, k19, puk2 sts in the gap, pm, and join for working in the round. *22 sts*

Both thumbs
Rounds 59-76: Follow chart, working decreases as indicated. *16 sts dec; 6 sts rem*
Break yarn, draw up through remaining 5 stitches, draw down through centre and fasten off to WS of work.

Make second mitten to match.

7 FINISHING

Weave in all ends to the back of the work, using yarn ends to carefully close any remaining gaps at the thumb base. Soak mittens in cool water for 20 minutes to allow stitches to relax and bloom. Press dry between towels. Shape mittens using glove blockers (if you have them) or pins to position thumb. Dry flat, and leave to fully dry.

Enjoy your Floral Tapestry mittens!

LEFT HAND CHART

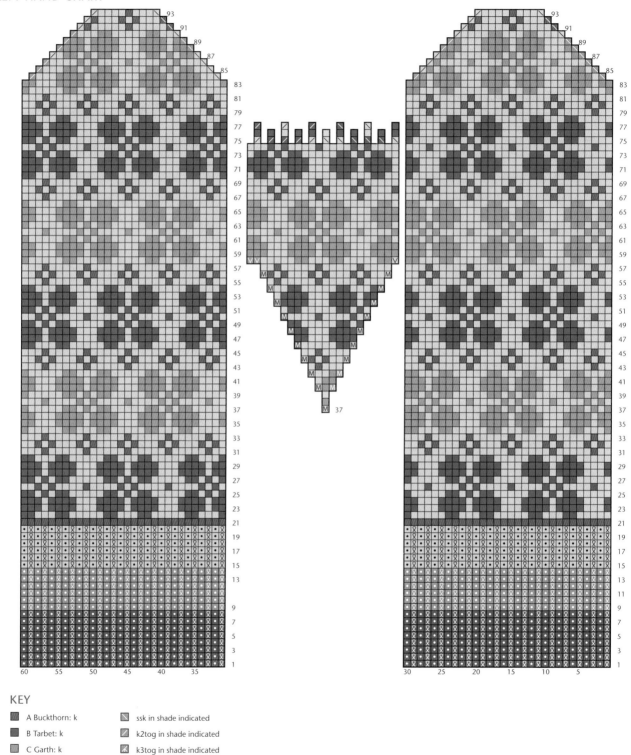

KEY

A Buckthorn: k		ssk in shade indicated	
B Tarbet: k		k2tog in shade indicated	
C Garth: k		k3tog in shade indicated	
A Smirr: k		m1 in shade indicated	
k1 tbl in shade indicated		puk 1 in shade indicated	
p in shade indicated		pattern repeat	

RIGHT HAND CHART

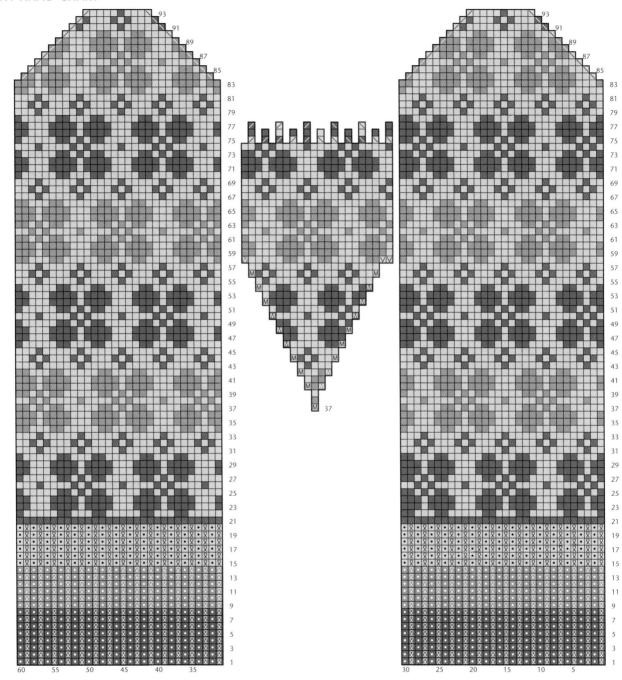

PATTERN REPEAT

81

MAJELLA

Many of my designs take their name from my Italian birthplace, among the Abruzzo. Majella is a massif rising to 2,795m that local people also refer to as 'Mother'. The surface texture of these mittens reminds me strongly of Majella clad in its vivid springtime hues. Linen stitch is ideal for a dense, warm mitten and this pattern is simply worked over two-round stripes of two alternating shades.

MAJELLA

YARN

Kate Davies Designs Àrd-Thìr (60% Peruvian Highland Wool; 40% Alpaca; 65m / 71yds per 50g skein)
A Vatersay: 2 x 50g skeins
B Luskentyre: 2 x 50g skeins

NEEDLES AND NOTIONS

Gauge-size needle(s) of your preferred type for working small circumferences
Below gauge-size needle(s) of your preferred type for working small circumferences
Waste yarn (for holding thumb stitches)
Stitch markers
Tapestry needle

GAUGE

19 sts and 32 rounds to 10cm /4in over linen-stitch pattern in the round on gauge-size needle(s)
Use 7mm needle(s) as a starting point for swatching.

SIZE

To fit adult hand with 18-20.5cm / 7-8in circumference

SPECIAL TECHNIQUES

Two-colour long-tail cast on
The following tutorial may be useful:
https://www.youtube.com/watch?v=JmsjGjCF4_E

PATTERN NOTES

These mittens are worked from bottom to top. After the cuff is worked in corrugated rib, the hand follows a striped linen stitch pattern. Waste yarn is inserted for an afterthought thumb, which is completed at the end.

INSTRUCTIONS

1 CAST ON, WORK CUFF

With shades A and B, below gauge-size needle(s) and using two-colour long-tail cast on (or your preferred method) cast on 38 sts, pm, and join for working in the round.
Rounds 1-12: (K1A, p1B) around.

2 WORK HAND

Change to gauge-size needle(s) and work set up round as foll:
Next round (round 13): (K1A, k1B) around.
Establish linen stitch pattern as foll:
Round 14: With A, (k1, sl1 wyif) around.
Round 15: With A, (sl1 wyif, k1) around.
Round 16: With B, (k1, sl1 wyif) around.
Round 17: With B, (sl1 wyif, k1) around.

Repeat rounds 14-17 3 more times. *29 rounds worked*

3 PLACE THUMB

Right Hand
Round 30: With A, k1, then with waste yarn, k6. Return these 6 sts to lh needle, then, with working yarn, work across these sts in pattern, and complete round as est.

Left Hand
Round 30: With A, (k1, sl1 wyif) 6 times, then with waste yarn, k6. Return these 6 sts to lh needle, then, with working yarn, work across these sts in pattern, and complete round as est

4 COMPLETE HAND

Round 31: As round 15.
Rounds 32 & 33: As rounds 16 and 17.
Rounds 34-57: Repeat rounds 14-17 6 times.
57 rounds worked

5 WORK MITTEN TOP

Maintaining 2-shade stripe pattern as est, decrease as foll:
Round 58: Ssk, (k1, sl1 wyif) 7 times, k1, k2tog, ssk, (sl1 wyif, k1) 7 times, sl1 wyif, k2tog. *4 sts dec; 34 sts rem*
Round 59: Ssk, (k1, sl1 wyif) 6 times, k1, k2tog, ssk, (sl1 wyif, k1) 6 times, sl1 wyif, k2tog. *4 sts dec; 30 sts rem*
Round 60: Ssk, (k1, sl1 wyif) 5 times, k1, k2tog, ssk, (sl1 wyif, k1) 5 times, sl1 wyif, k2tog. *4 sts dec; 26 sts rem*
Round 61: Ssk, (k1, sl1 wyif) 4 times, k1, k2tog, ssk, (sl1 wyif, k1) 4 times, sl1 wyif, k2tog. *4 sts dec; 22 sts rem*
Round 62: Ssk, (k1, sl1 wyif) 3 times, k1, k2tog, ssk, (sl1 wyif, k1) 3 times, sl1 wyif, k2tog. *4 sts dec; 18 sts rem*
Round 63: Ssk, (k1, sl1 wyif) twice, k1, k2tog, ssk, (sl1 wyif, k1) twice, sl1 wyif, k2tog. *4 sts dec; 14 sts rem*
Break A. With B graft together 2 sets of 7sts.

6 COMPLETE THUMB

Carefully remove waste yarn and sl12 sts to gauge-size needle(s).
Round 1: Join in B, *puk2 sts in the gap where thumb meets palm, (sl1 wyif, k1) 3 times; repeat from * once. *16 sts*
Round 2: Join in A, (k1, sl1 wyif) around.
Round 3: (Sl1 wyif, k1) around.
Round 4: With B, repeat round 2.
Round 5: Repeat round 3.
Rounds 6-17: Repeat rounds 2-5 3 more times.
Round 18: Ssk, (k1, sl1 wyif) twice, k2tog, ssk, (k1, sl1 wyif) twice, k2tog. *4 sts dec; 12 sts rem*
Round 19: (Ssk, sl1 wyif, k1, k2tog) twice. *4 sts dec; 8 sts rem*
Round 20: (Ssk, k2tog) twice. *4 sts dec; 4 sts rem*
Break yarn. Draw up through remaining 4 sts, draw down and fasten off to WS of work.
Make a second mitten to match.

7 FINISHING

Weave in all ends to the back of the work, using yarn ends to carefully close any remaining gaps at thumb base. Soak mittens in cool water for 20 minutes to allow stitches to relax and bloom. Press dry between towels. Shape mittens using glove blockers (if you have them) or pins to position thumb. Dry flat, and leave to fully dry.

Enjoy your Majella mittens!

BROKEN
HERRINGBONE

This cosy snood, worked in two tonally similar shades, is based on a repetitive motif similar to a hashtag, with three horizontal and three vertical lines. When knitted, the final visual effect is reminiscent of a herringbone, that's been broken in regular sections. The motif works by shifting one stitch in both horizontal and vertical directions, and the resulting square motif is quite wide: 133 stitches and 133 rounds - all of which are charted here. The snood can be worn long, or wrapped twice around the neck.

BROKEN HERRINGBONE

YARN

Kate Davies Designs Milarrochy Tweed (70% Wool; 30% Mohair; 100m / 109yds per 25g ball)
A Gloamin': 6 x 25g balls
B Campion: 6 x 25g balls

NEEDLES AND NOTIONS

2 gauge-size needles of your preferred type for working in the round
Stitch markers
Tapestry needle
Waste yarn (for provisional cast on)

GAUGE

32 stitches and 36 rounds to 10cm / 4in over stranded stockinette in the round on gauge-size needle(s)
Use 3mm needle(s) as a starting point for swatching.

SIZE

One size to be wrapped loosely twice around the neck.
Final measurements after blocking:
Height: 20cm / 7¾in
Length: 166cm / 65½in

PATTERN NOTES

After a provisional cast on, the colourwork is worked as one long tube, which is grafted and joined at the end.

SPECIAL TECHNIQUES

Provisional cast on
Use a crochet provisional cast on, or your preferred method. The following tutorial may be useful:
https://kddandco.com/tutorials/crochet-provisional-cast-on-tutorial

Grafting
The following tutorial may be useful:
https://www.youtube.com/watch?v=ZhFbOA0E4Eo

CHART NOTES

The chart looks more complex than it is in actuality. A particular bonus of this pattern is that it is very easy to spot mistakes!

INSTRUCTIONS

1 CAST ON

With waste yarn, gauge-size needle(s), and using your preferred provisional cast on method, cast on 133 sts, pm, and join for working in the round.
Set up round: Join in A and k 1 round.

2 WORK SNOOD

Rounds 1-133: Join in B, and, reading chart from right to left and changing shades where indicated, work chart rounds 1-133.
Repeat rounds 1-133 3 times more.
Repeat rounds 1-60 once more. *592 rounds worked*
Break B. Weave in all ends to the back of the work.

3 GRAFT SNOOD ENDS

Break A leaving a tail 4 times longer than snood circumference.
Carefully remove the provisional cast on and slip 133 sts onto a second circular needle. Place needles parallel to one another and, with A, graft the two ends of the snood together. Break A and weave in end to snood interior.

4 FINISHING

Soak snood in cool water for 20 minutes to allow stitches to relax and bloom. Press dry between towels. Shape snood, using blocking pads and pins, leave to fully dry.

Enjoy your Broken Herringbone snood!

CHART

KEY

A Gloamin:' k

B Campion: k

pattern repeat

PATTERN REPEAT

H Y P N O

I love geometric shapes, especially when rendered in monochrome shades of black and grey. I called this design 'Hypno' as decentering the smaller squares of each repeat gives a slight hypnotic feeling. You can choose to knit the Hypno mittens, or fingerless gloves . . . or both!

HYPNO

YARN
Kate Davies Designs Milarrochy Tweed (70% Wool; 30% Mohair; 100m / 109yds per 25g ball)
A Bruce: 2 x 25g balls (mittens); 1 x 25g ball (fingerless gloves)
B Birkin: 1 x 25g ball (mittens); 2 x 25g balls (fingerless gloves)

NEEDLES AND NOTIONS
Gauge-size needle(s) of your preferred type for working small circumferences
Below gauge-size needle(s) of your preferred type for working small circumferences
Gauge-size needle(s) of your preferred type for working fingers
Long gauge-size circular needles or holder for holding finger stitches
Waste yarn (for holding thumb stitches)
Stitch markers
Tapestry needle

GAUGE
32 stitches and 36 rounds to 10cm / 4in over stranded colourwork in the round on gauge-size needle(s)
Use 3mm needle(s) as a starting point for swatching.

SIZE
Both the mittens and fingerless gloves are fairly large-fitting, designed to comfortably fit hands with 21-22cm / 8-9in circumference. The mittens can be worn by smaller hands fitting as a cosy outer layer over another pair of mitts or gloves.

SPECIAL TECHNIQUES
Long-tail tubular-cast on
The following tutorial may be useful:
http://dyedreams.blogspot.com/2009/03/tubular-cast-on-in-round-for-socks.html

PATTERN NOTES
These mittens (or fingerless gloves) are worked from bottom to top. The cuff is worked in 1x1 rib in alternating shades, then the hand is worked in stranded colourwork, inserting waste yarn for an afterthought thumb. After the hand is completed, the top is finished with mitten shaping or half fingers, and the thumb is worked separately.

CHART NOTES
The chart includes cuff, thumb placement and each side of the hand. Take care to place thumb correctly for the left and right hands and read the chart from right to left throughout.

INSTRUCTIONS: Mittens

1
CAST ON, WORK CUFF

With shade A, below gauge-size needle(s), and using 1x1 long-tail tubular-cast on (or your preferred method) cast on 66 sts, pm, and join for working in the round.
Rounds 1-2: Reading chart from right to left, work in 1x1 rib as foll:
(K1, p1) around.
Round 3: Join in B and continue to work in 1x1 rib as foll:
(K1A, p1B) around.
Changing shades to work offset rib as indicated, work chart rounds 4-18.

2
WORK HAND

Change to gauge-size needle(s), and, working chart from right to left and changing shades where indicated work chart rounds 19-44.

3
PLACE THUMB

Right Hand
Round 45: K1 in pattern, k10 with waste yarn, return last 10 sts to lh needle, then, with working yarn, work across these sts in pattern, and complete round as est.

Left Hand
Round 45: K22 in pattern, k10 with waste yarn, return last 10 sts to lh needle then, with working yarn, work across these sts in pattern, and complete round as est.

4
COMPLETE HAND

Rounds 46-84: Work from chart.

5
WORK MITTEN TOP

Rounds 85-95: Follow chart, working decreases as indicated. *44 sts dec; 22 sts rem*
Break A. With B graft together 2 sets of 11 sts. Break B.

6
COMPLETE THUMB

With A and gauge-size needle(s) work thumb as foll:

Carefully remove waste yarn, and sl20 sts to gauge-size needles.

Round 46: K10, puk2 sts in the gap where thumb meets palm, k10, puk2 sts in the gap, pm, and join for working in the round. *24 sts*
Rounds 47-70: K24.
Round 71: (K2tog) around. *12 sts dec; 12 sts rem*
Round 72: K12.
Round 73: (K2tog) around. *6 sts dec; 6 sts rem*
Round 74: K6.
Break yarn. Thread yarn through remaining 6 sts and fasten off to WS.

Make a second mitten to match.

7
FINISHING

Weave in all ends to the back of the work, using yarn ends to carefully close any remaining gaps at thumb base. Soak mittens in cool water for 20 minutes to allow stitches to relax and bloom. Press dry between towels. Shape mittens using glove blockers (if you have them) or pins to position thumb. Dry flat, and leave to fully dry.

Enjoy your Hypno mittens!

INSTRUCTIONS: Fingerless Gloves

WORK STEPS 1-3 AS FOR HYPNO MITTENS

4

WORK HAND

Rounds 46-73: Work in pattern.
Break yarn A.

5

WORK HALF FINGERS

Right Hand
Index Finger
With B and gauge-size needle(s), work index finger as foll:
Round 1: K10, using backward-loop cast on, cast on 1 st in the gap between fingers, sl23 sts to holder or spare needle (palm), sl23 sts to a second holder (back of hand), k10, pm, and join for working in the round. *21 sts*
Rounds 2-11: K21.
Round 12: Bind off. Break yarn.

Middle Finger
With B and gauge-size needle(s), work middle finger as foll:
Round 1: Sl8 sts from palm sts holder, k8, using backward-loop cast on, cast on 1 st in the gap between fingers, sl8 sts from back of hand sts holder, k8, using backward-loop cast on, cast on 1 st in the gap between fingers, pm, and join for working in the round. *18 sts*
Rounds 2-11: K18.
Round 12: Bind off. Break yarn.

Ring Finger
With B and gauge-size needle(s), work ring finger as foll:
Round 1: Sl8 sts from palm sts holder, k8, using backward-loop cast on, cast on 1 st in the gap between fingers, sl8 sts from back of hand sts holder, k8, using backward-loop cast on, cast on 1 st in the gap between fingers, pm, and join for working in the round. *18 sts*
Rounds 2-11: K18.
Round 12: Bind off. Break yarn.

Little Finger
With B and gauge-size needle(s), work little finger as foll:
Round 1: Sl7 sts from palm sts holder, k7, sl7 sts from back of hand sts holder, k7, using backward-loop cast on, cast on 2 sts in the gap between fingers, pm, and join for working in the round. *16 sts*
Rounds 2-11: K16.
Round 12: Bind off. Break yarn.

Left Hand
Little Finger
With B and gauge-size needle(s), work little finger as foll:
Round 1: K7, using backward-loop cast on, cast on 2 sts in the gap between fingers, sl26 sts to holder or spare needle (palm), sl26 sts to a second holder or spare needle (back of hand), k7, pm, and join for working in the round. *16 sts*
Rounds 2-11: K16.
Round 12: Bind off. Break yarn.

Ring Finger
With B and gauge-size needle(s), work ring finger as foll:
Round 1: Sl8 sts from palm sts holder, k8, using backward-loop cast on, cast on 1 st in the gap between fingers, sl8 sts from back of hand sts holder, k8, using backward-loop cast on, cast on 1 st in the gap between fingers, pm, and join for working in the round. *18 sts*
Rounds 2-11: K18.
Round 12: Bind off. Break yarn.

Middle Finger
With B and gauge-size needle(s), work middle finger as foll:
Round 1: Sl8 sts from palm sts holder, k8, using backward-loop cast on, cast on 1 st in the gap between fingers, sl8 sts from back of hand sts holder, k8, using backward-loop cast on, cast on 1 st in the gap between fingers, pm, and join for working in the round. *18 sts*
Rounds 2-11: K18.
Round 12: Bind off. Break yarn.

Index Finger
With B and gauge-size needle(s), work index finger as foll:
Round 1: Sl the last 10 sts from palm sts holder, k10, sl the last 10 sts from back of hand sts holder, k10, using backward-loop cast on, cast on 1 st in the gap between fingers, pm, and join for working in the round. *21 sts*
Rounds 2-11: K21.
Round 12: Bind off. Break yarn.

6

COMPLETE THUMB

Carefully remove waste yarn and sl20 sts to gauge-size needle(s).
Round 1: With B, k10, puk2 sts in the gap where thumb meets palm, k10, puk2 sts in the gap, pm, and join for working in the round. *24 sts*
Rounds 2-11: K24.
Round 12: Bind off. Break yarn

Make a second fingerless glove to match.

7

FINISHING

Weave in all ends to the back of the work, using yarn ends to carefully close any remaining gaps at the base of fingers and thumb. Soak gloves in cool water for 20 minutes to allow stitches to relax and bloom. Press dry between towels. Shape gloves using glove blockers (you'll find a handy template at the end of this pattern) or pins to position thumb and fingers. Dry flat, and leave to fully dry.

Enjoy your Hypno fingerless gloves!

CHART

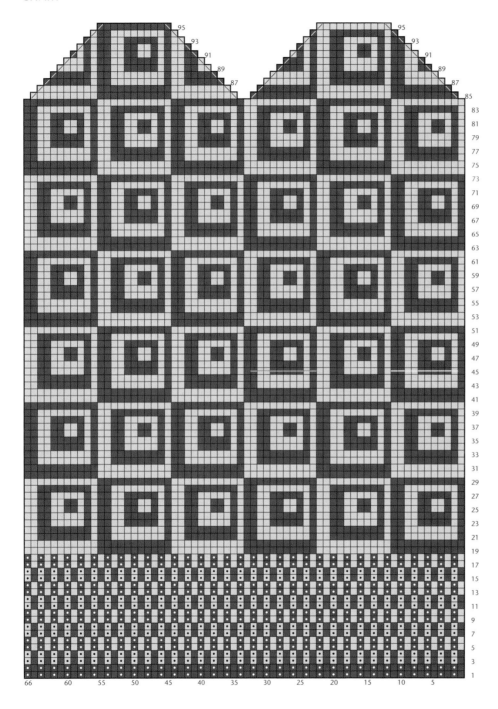

KEY

■ A Bruce: k

□ B Birkin: k

☐ p in shade indicated

◩ ssk in shade indicated

◪ k2tog in shade indicated

▤ k with waste yarn, then
in shade indicated (left hand)

▤ k with waste yarn, the
in shade indicated (right hand)

□ pattern repeat

73 mitt top / dividing round

PATTERN REPEAT

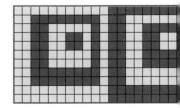

Overleaf you'll find two sets of templates to make blockers for gloves, mittens and fingerless gloves, in sizes S/M and M/L. Simply copy and cut out the shapes from EVA interlocking foam tiles.

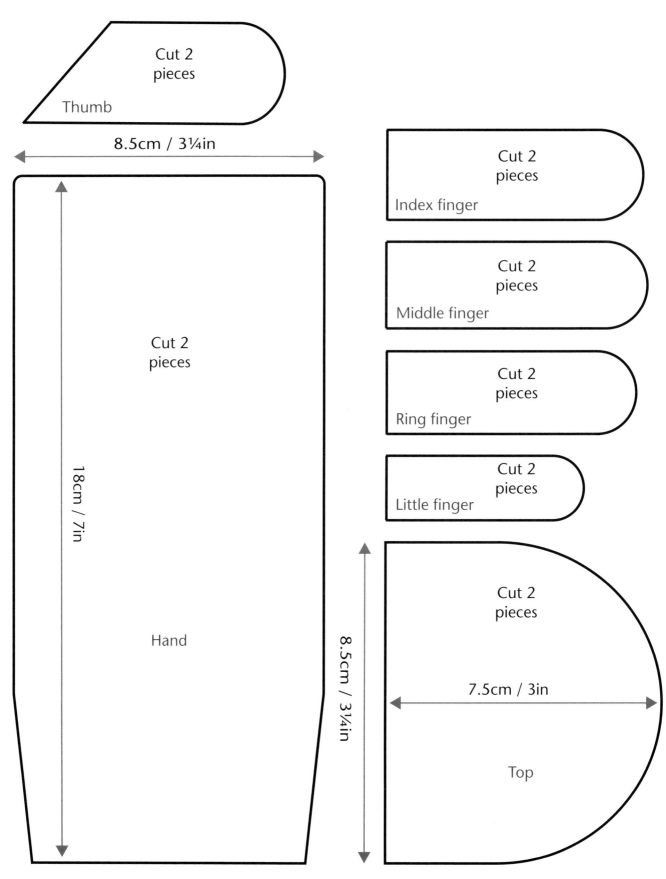

Thumb

Cut 2
pieces

8.5cm / 3¼in

Cut 2
pieces

Hand

18cm / 7in

Cut 2
pieces

Index finger

Cut 2
pieces

Middle finger

Cut 2
pieces

Ring finger

Cut 2
pieces

Little finger

8.5cm / 3¼in

Cut 2
pieces

Top

7.5cm / 3in

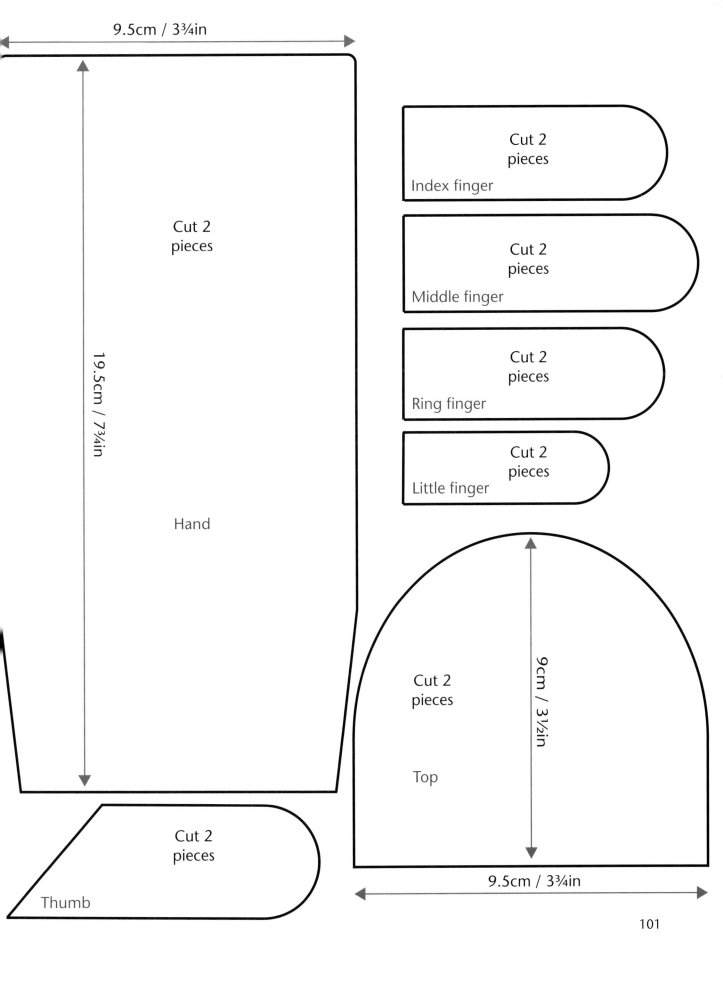

9.5cm / 3¾in

Cut 2
pieces

19.5cm / 7¾in

Hand

Cut 2
pieces

Index finger

Cut 2
pieces

Middle finger

Cut 2
pieces

Ring finger

Cut 2
pieces

Little finger

Cut 2
pieces

9cm / 3½in

Top

Cut 2
pieces

Thumb

9.5cm / 3¾in

RESOURCES

SPECIAL TECHNIQUES
Special techniques are described in each individual pattern, with links to useful online tutorials where relevant.

A NOTE ON GAUGE AND SWATCHING
Whichever needle gives you the specified gauge is your 'gauge-size' needle. You'll usually select the size immediately below for your 'below gauge-size' needle, or above for your 'above gauge-size' needle unless differently instructed. Don't rely on your instincts ('I always knit with this yarn on an xx needle'), and please don't simply start knitting with the needle upon which gauge was achieved in the sample (which is included in the pattern only for reference, and as a starting point for swatching). Please bear in mind that individual knitting styles and gauges can vary widely.

FIND CLAUDIA
Website: www.klakladesigns.com
E-mail: claudia@klakladesigns.com
Social Media: @klakladesigns on Twitter, Instagram and Facebook, and as klakla on Ravelry

KDD RAVELRY GROUP
To seek help with any of the patterns in this book, or to chat with your fellow knitters, join us in the lively and supportive KDD Ravelry group:
https://www.ravelry.com/groups/kdd--co

NEED YARN?
You'll find supplies of the Milarrochy Tweed and Àrd-Thìr yarns featured in this book in the KDD shop:
https://www.shopkdd.com

FURTHER READING
While working on these designs, I drew inspiration and encouragement from the essays in Kate's book *Wheesht.*
Kate Davies, *Wheesht: Creative Making in Uncertain Times* (2019)
Margaret Radcliffe, *The Knitting Answer Book* (2006)
Montse Stanley, *Knitter's Handbook* (2001 edn)
Elizabeth Zimmermann, *Knitting Without Tears* (1971)

THE COLOUR MOVES TEAM
Design: Claudia Fiocchetti
Editor, styling: Kate Davies
Photography, graphic design: Tom Barr
Technical editing: Frauke Urban
Copy-editing: Ivor Normand
Proof-reading: Sarah Mackay
Studio assistance: Sam Kilday
Models: Jane Hunter, Fenella Pole, Sam Kilday

Shot on location by Loch Lomond and at the KDD studio, Glasgow, Scotland.